GREGG SHORTHAND SIMPLIFIED

FOR COLLEGES   *Volume Two*

LOUIS A. LESLIE

Coauthor Simplified Revision of Gregg Shorthand

CHARLES E. ZOUBEK

Coauthor Simplified Revision of Gregg Shorthand

RUSSELL J. HOSLER

Professor, University of Wisconsin, Madison, Wisconsin

GREGG   PUBLISHING   DIVISION

McGraw-Hill Book Company, Inc.

NEW YORK   CHICAGO   SAN FRANCISCO   DALLAS   TORONTO   LONDON

Shorthand Plates Written by

Charles Rader

PUBLISHED BY GREGG PUBLISHING DIVISION

McGraw-Hill Book Company, Inc.
Printed in the United States of America

PREFACE

Gregg Shorthand Simplified for Colleges, Volume Two, is designed to achieve three major purposes: (1) to provide a constant, automatic review of the theory of Gregg Shorthand Simplified presented in Volume One; (2) to develop the student's shorthand speed; and (3) to lay a foundation for accurate, rapid transcription.

The material in this volume is divided into sixteen chapters, each chapter consisting of five lessons. A typical lesson in Part I (Lessons 1 through 40) contains a series of carefully planned word lists built around word families, brief-form derivatives, frequent business-letter phrases, word beginnings and endings, and the major principles of Gregg Shorthand Simplified. It also contains 800 to 1,000 words of carefully selected practice material in shorthand.

In Part II (Lessons 41 through 80) a typical lesson is organized on the same lines as those of the lessons in Part I, with the exception that a new feature — Preview and Writing Practice — is added. In this new feature, 150 to 300 words of business-letter material are given in *type*, preceded by a shorthand preview.

To provide the most effective intensive review, the word and phrase lists in each chapter of *Gregg Shorthand Simplified for Colleges,* Volume Two, are organized as follows:

1. The first lesson contains a number of word families, which enable the student to take the fullest advantage of the principle of analogy in word construction.

2. The second lesson contains a series of brief-form derivatives followed by geographical expressions.

3. The third lesson contains useful business-letter phrases based on a study of more than 250,000 running words of business material, arranged in analogical groupings.

4. The fourth lesson contains a number of word beginnings or word endings.

5. The fifth lesson contains lists of illustrations of the major word-building principles of Gregg Shorthand Simplified.

To give the student a sampling of the type of vocabulary used in some of the major fields of business activity and also to add interest to his study, each chapter in *Gregg Shorthand Simplified for Colleges,* Volume Two, is built around the correspondence of a specific field.

In *Gregg Shorthand Simplified for Colleges,* Volume One, eleven of the simplest pretranscription factors are presented. These eleven factors are reviewed throughout the eighty lessons of Volume Two. In addition, beginning with Lesson 11, eighteen new and more advanced factors of transcription are included in each lesson.

Gregg Shorthand Simplified for Colleges is a distinctive contribution to the teaching of shorthand. Special acknowledgment is made of the suggestions of scores of shorthand teachers and the assistance of Professor Clyde I. Blanchard, University of Tulsa, Tulsa, Oklahoma, in developing this new college-level shorthand program. In the preparation of this volume the authors have skillfully combined their rich teaching and writing experience, Mr. Leslie and Mr. Zoubek being coauthors of the Simplified Revision of Gregg Shorthand, and Doctor Hosler an active college-level shorthand teacher.

Gregg Shorthand Simplified for Colleges is offered to the teaching profession with particular pride and satisfaction. It is the first shorthand program of its type to be published. Following the completion of the theory of Gregg Shorthand Simplified in Volume One, this text, Volume Two, makes a gradual and substantial contribution to the student's shorthand skill. Additional texts are available for the development of more advanced skill in writing and transcribing shorthand.

THE PUBLISHERS

PART I

CHAPTERS 1-8

CHAPTER I

LESSON 1

1. WORD FAMILIES

-FORM

-TAKE

-SOME

-THING

-COME

Key

Form, conform, reform, uniform, perform, misinform, deform.
Take, overtake, undertake, partake, retake, mistake.
Some, lonesome, wholesome, tiresome, handsome, bothersome.
Thing, anything, everything, something, nothing, plaything, things.
Come, become, outcome, welcome, overcome, income.

CHAPTER I

READING AND WRITING PRACTICE

2.

terrified
men's

well-read
hyphenated
before noun

, series
cheating
, conjunction

neighborhood
, *when* clause

, series
surprised

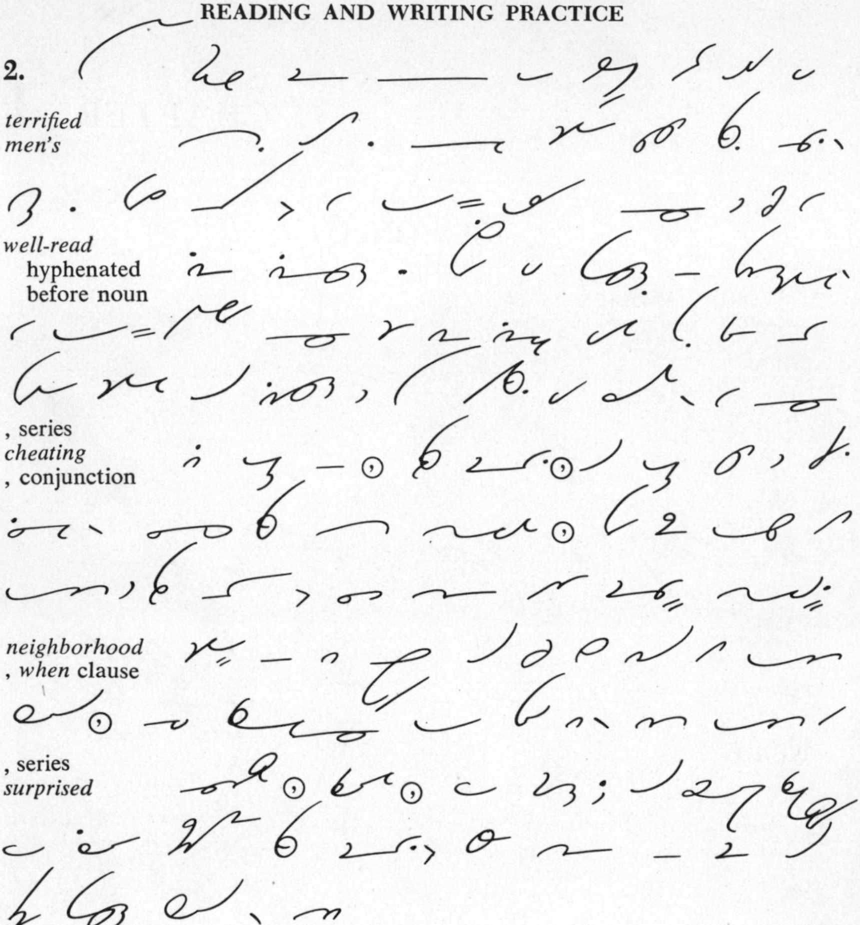

3.

fitted
, introductory

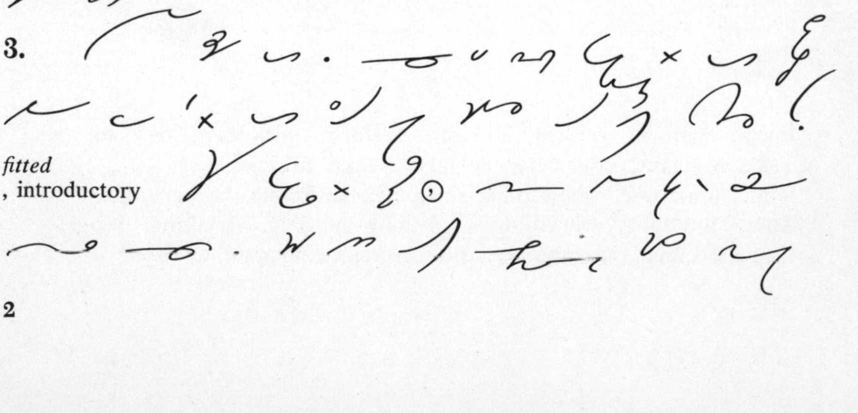

, introductory
reasonable

50/-

4.

, parenthetical
, introductory
Furthermore
matched

5.

, *when* clause
engagement

CHAPTER I

, *if* clause
first aid

6.

Occasionally
embarrassed

, introductory
oblige
visitor
rejoicing)

similar
, *if* clause

7.

, *as* clause
Christmas
until

8:30

8:30

, introductory

idea
, parenthetical
remain

, *if clause*
leisurely

8.

anniversary
, apposition
, introductory

, *if clause*
thrifty
soul

9.

, *if clause*
clothing
, apposition

well known
no noun,
no hyphen
men's
, conjunction

10.

, parenthetical
minds

materials
, conjunction

, introductory
repeat
welcome
source

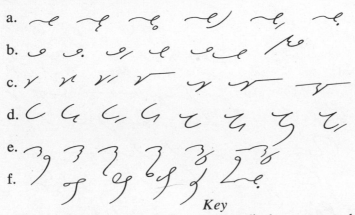

LESSON 2

11. BRIEF-FORM DERIVATIVES

a.

b.

c.

d.

e.

f.

Key

a. Correspond, corresponds, correspondingly, correspondent, corresponded, corresponding.

b. Regard, regarding, regarded, regards, regardless, disregard.

c. State, states, stated, statement, restate, restatement, misstatement.

d. Present, presents, presented, presentation, represent, representation, representative, represented.

e. Consider, considers, considerable, considerably, considerate, inconsiderate.

f. Ever, whenever, wherever, whatever, whichever, ever-increasing.

12. GEOGRAPHICAL EXPRESSIONS

a.

b.

c.

Key

a. Stamford, Hartford, Bradford, Cranford, Bedford, Oxford.

b. Maine, New Hampshire, Virginia, Massachusetts, Connecticut, Rhode Island, New Jersey, New York.

c. United States, United States of America, England, Canada, Mexico, Guam, Hawaii.

7

CHAPTER I

READING AND WRITING PRACTICE

13.

, *when* clause
, series
tangible
possessions

, parenthetical
, apposition
appearance

well dressed
no noun,
no hyphen

up-to-date
hyphenated
before noun

14.

, parenthetical
regardless
, introductory

experience
guide
, *if* clause
, parenthetical

15.

men's
clothing

, conjunction
, parenthetical
, introductory

16.

, conjunction
otherwise

CHAPTER I

, introductory
warned

, introductory

, introductory
alterations

, introductory
gamble

[Shorthand notation - Gregg shorthand]

, conjunction
, introductory
, *if* clause

, parenthetical
skeptics

, *if* clause
earliest
opportunity

17.

, *as* clause
financial
axiom

, introductory
, parenthetical

bargain
, parenthetical

, conjunction
whole
, parenthetical

CHAPTER I

, introductory
customers

, series

overcoats
, introductory

, *if* clause

convenience

LESSON 3

18. Useful Business-Letter Phrases

I

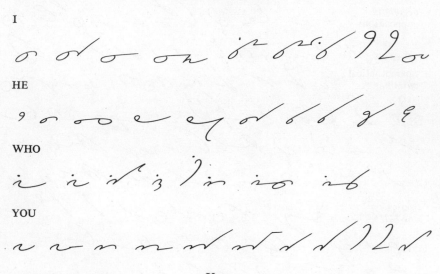

HE

WHO

YOU

Key

I can, I could, I am, I am sure, I do not, I do not think, I did, I have, I have not, I know.

He is, he can, he may, he will, he will be, he could, he would, he did, he said, he was.

Who will, who are, who desire, who is, who have, who can, who make, who made.

You are, you are not, you can, you cannot, you could, you could not, you would, you did, you have, you have not, you do.

19. Frequent Names

a.

b.

Key

a. Adams, Anderson, Baker, Barry, Becker, Bennett, Brennan, Brown.

b. Adeline, Agnes, Amelia, Annabell, Augusta, Barbara.

13

CHAPTER I

READING AND WRITING PRACTICE

20.

beginning
, apposition

, parenthetical
customer

, series
one-half

21.

well known
  no noun,
  no hyphen
, introductory

109

, if clause
dangerous
tears

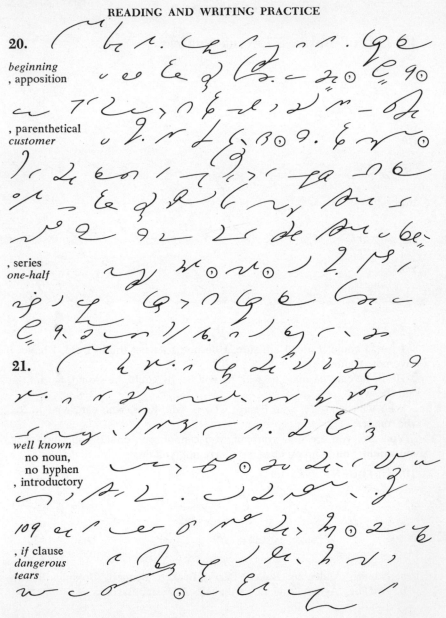

(shorthand outlines)

, introductory
worrying

22.

accede
accept

two-week
    hyphenated
    before noun
, introductory

length
, *if* clause

23.

, *introductory*
features

, *if clause*
breakfast

24.

: *pleasure*
, *introductory*

, *if clause*
messenger

, *introductory*
, *when* clause

major
, *if clause*

25.
soliciting
negotiations
furriers

, conjunction
drastic

styling
quality
substantial

, parenthetical
dissatisfaction

wholesaler's
comparable

, if clause
racks

26.

, introductory
tempting
introductory

, apposition
costumes

well-rounded
hyphenated
before noun

theater
, series

, as clause
hurry

LESSON 4

27. WORD BEGINNINGS

AFTER-

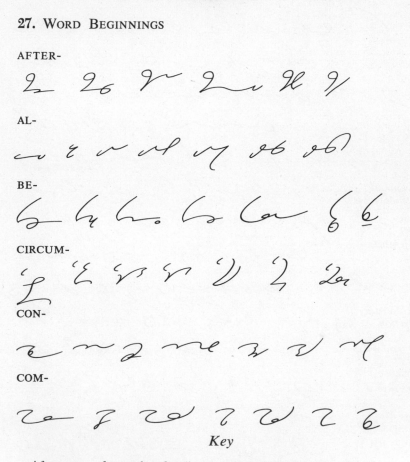

AL-

BE-

CIRCUM-

CON-

COM-

Key

Afternoon, aftermath, afterdinner, afterglow, aftertaste, afterward.
Almost, also, alter, alteration, alterable, alternate, alternative.
Became, because, becomingly, begin, belittle, beside, beware.
Circumnavigate, circumspect, circumstances, circumstantial, circumvent, circumvention, circumference.
Conceal, concur, confine, congress, consult, consistent, contribute.
Compliment, compete, complaint, compose, comprehend, compound, compare.

READING AND WRITING PRACTICE

28.

, introductory
Comfort

skilled
machinery
, introductory

, parenthetical
pair

, introductory
collection

, *if* clause
wearing

29.

patience
, series

worry
, parenthetical

[Shorthand content]

worn
, introductory

30.
, *if* clause
sensible
height

, introductory
, series
posture

self-consciousness
self-assurance

31.

CHAPTER I

publicity
passed
materials

, introductory
benefit
effect

, introductory

, parenthetical
belief
today's

, when clause

32.

, introductory
youngster

, parenthetical
, as clause

22

(shorthand outlines)

33.

man's
wardrobe
bears

leather
, apposition

34.
, introductory
thousands
offhand

volume
20 per cent

ladies'

CHAPTER I

well built
no noun,
no hyphen
, conjunction

summarize
, introductory

, introductory
profit

grateful
, conjunction

35.

whether
anyone

, parenthetical
advice

LESSON 5

36. Word-Building Practice—Diphthongs

I

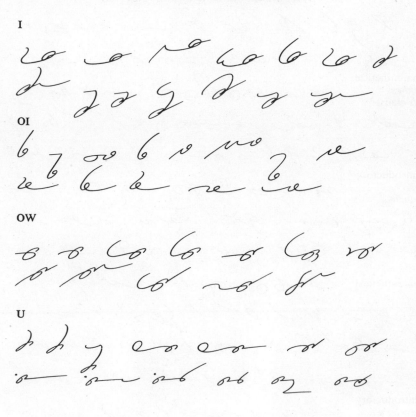

OI

OW

U

Key

Flight, light, delight, polite, bright, fright, fight, vital, invite, insight, provide, divide, recite, recital.

Joy, enjoy, annoy, boy, toy, destroy, convoy, toil, soil, boil, foil, coil, loyal.

Now, cow, plow, brow, mouth, blouse, scout, doubt, doubtless, proud, cloud, powder.

Few, view, review, argue, argument, cute, acute, human, humor, humid, unit, uniform, unite.

READING AND WRITING PRACTICE

37. Science and the Traveler

[Shorthand content]

, parenthetical
clothes
, *as* clause

, introductory
career
launched

, parenthetical

, introductory
traveler's
necessity

lengthy
, series

, parenthetical

awakens
, *when* clause
, introductory

scarcely

, conjunction
, *as* clause

carried
, introductory

, *if* clause
leisurely
, parenthetical

CHAPTER I

two-week
   hyphenated
   before noun
, parenthetical

week-long
   hyphenated
   before noun
, parenthetical

, introductory
imperative

, introductory
, parenthetical
consequently

28

science
, introductory

overnight

, introductory

incredible
, parenthetical

, introductory
ironing

, series
rinse

CHAPTER I

[shorthand content]

old-fashioned
reasonably

, introductory
carrying

article
, parenthetical

, introductory
nuclear

–Louis A. Leslie

LESSON 6

38. WORD FAMILIES

-LONG

-SIGN

-LET

-SURE

-SERVE

Key

Long, belong, prolong, headlong, oblong, along.
Sign, assign, design, resign, countersign, assignment, designer.
Outlet, pamphlet, bracelet, booklet, inlet, violet.
Insure, assure, treasure, measure, pleasure, reassure.
Serve, deserve, conserve, observe, preserve, reserve, deservedly.

READING AND WRITING PRACTICE

39.

340

husband
, parenthetical

silverware
container

worth while
  no noun,
  no hyphen

40.

happiness
family

efficiently
, introductory

, when clause
convinced

, apposition

Cordially

41.

choice
majority

, *if clause*
grateful

easy-to-understand
  hyphenated
  before noun
Yours

42.
Sometime
natural
, *introductory*

CHAPTER II

, introductory
adjustments
appliances

, introductory
preliminary

, introductory

43.

yours
, *if* clause

, series
cheery

remodeling
, *if* clause

34

44.

wife's

instructions
amateur

self-addressed
, conjunction

45.

, introductory
ironing

part-time
    hyphenated
    before noun
, *if* clause

[shorthand]

2121
, introductory
, conjunction
equipped

[shorthand]

46.

glance
enclosed

[shorthand]

premises
, *as* clause

[shorthand]

, introductory

[shorthand]

7777

[shorthand]

LESSON 7

47. Brief-Form Derivatives

a.
b.
c.
d.
e.
f.

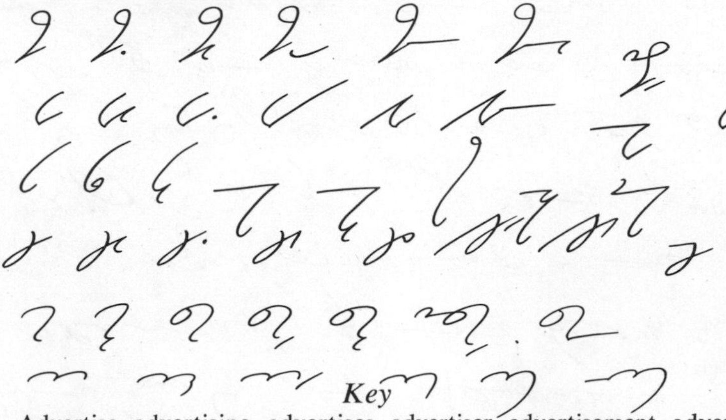

Key

a. Advertise, advertising, advertises, advertiser, advertisement, advertisements, unadvertised.

b. Part, parts, parting, parted, depart, department, impart, apart.

c. Body, bodily, bodies, embody, embodies, everybody, nobody, somebody.

d. Satisfy, satisfies, satisfying, satisfaction, satisfactorily, dissatisfied, dissatisfaction, unsatisfactory.

e. Company, companies, accompany, accompanied, accompanies, unaccompanied, accompaniment.

f. Conclude, concludes, concluded, conclusion, conclusive, inconclusive.

48. Geographical Expressions

a.
b.
c.

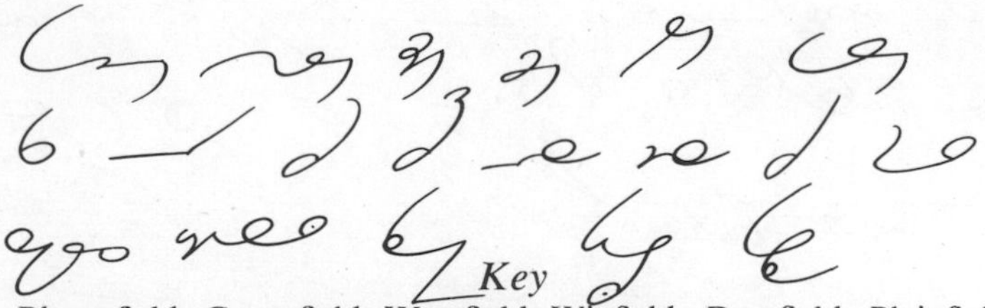

Key

a. Bloomfield, Greenfield, Westfield, Winfield, Deerfield, Plainfield.

b. Pennsylvania, Maryland, Virginia, West Virginia, North Carolina, South Carolina, Georgia, Florida.

c. Argentina, Australia, Belgium, Bolivia, Brazil.

CHAPTER II

READING AND WRITING PRACTICE

49.

today's
identical
, introductory

, parenthetical
distinctive

, when clause
major

its
attractive

everyone
, as clause

50.

planning
, introductory

unusual
surface

, conjunction

51.
planning
, *if* clause
, apposition

, series

describes
advantages

52.

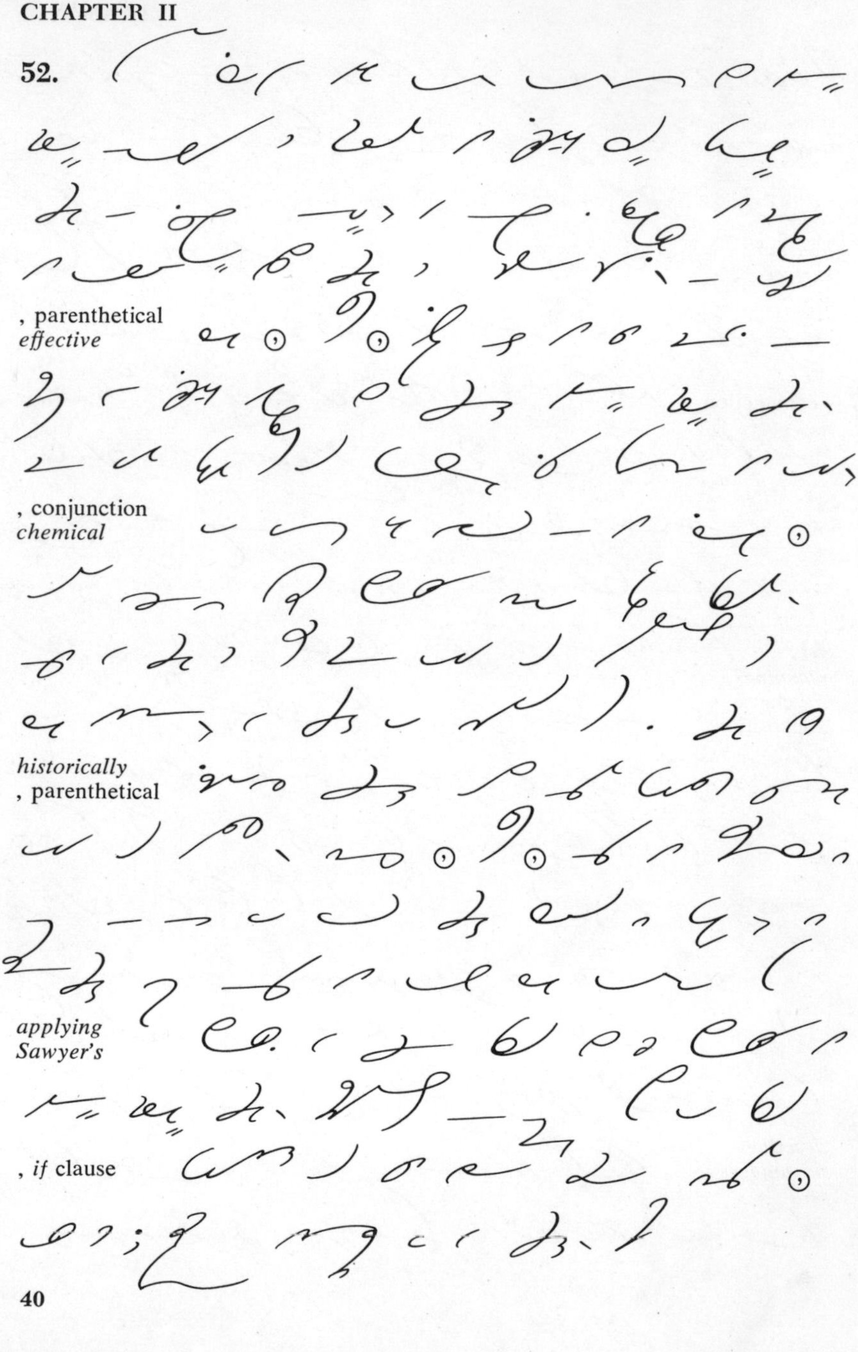

, parenthetical
effective

, conjunction
chemical

historically
, parenthetical

applying
Sawyer's

, *if* clause

53.

, introductory
available

pictures
immediately

disturbing
odors

demonstrate

54.

attractively
, *when* clause

well known
no noun,
no hyphen

, introductory
entirely

, introductory
recommend

, conjunction
guarantee
weather

, introductory

, introductory
prepared

, *if* clause
guide
forwarded

LESSON 8

55. USEFUL BUSINESS-LETTER PHRASES

THEY

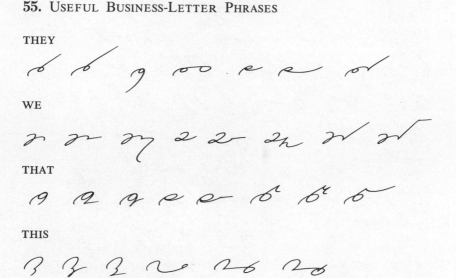

WE

THAT

THIS

Key

They would, they did, they have, they may, they are, they will, they could.

We can, we cannot, we cannot be, we are, we are not, we are sure, we could, we could not.

That is, that is not, that is the, that are, that are not, that it is, that it was, that it will.

This is, this is the, this is not, this letter, this matter, this might.

56. FREQUENT NAMES

a.

b.

Key

a. Burke, Callahan, Cameron, Campbell, Carroll.

b. Abraham, Adam, Adolph, Albert, Alfred, Andrew.

CHAPTER II

READING AND WRITING PRACTICE

57.

well-kept
hyphenated
before noun

, parenthetical
repairs

, parenthetical
inventory

maintenance
well trained
no noun,
no hyphen

, *if* clause
competent
surveyor

44

58.

, parenthetical
worries

fuel
dependable
delivery

, introductory
families
switching

, *if* clause
survey

, parenthetical
, introductory

CHAPTER II

, series
economically
engineers

59.

, introductory
annual
arrangement

, conjunction
frequently
overlooked

interruptions
inconveniences

patronage
, series

46

questions
, if clause

60.

fall's
assurance

, introductory
, parenthetical

thorough
overhauling

, if clause
installed

efficient
, when clause

, if clause
enclosed

61.

, as clause
, apposition

, parenthetical
guarantee
materials

lack
, introductory

, parenthetical

, if clause

LESSON 9

62. Word Endings

-ALLY, -ILY

-LY

-CIAL, -TIAL

-FUL

-IFY

-BLE

Key

Finally, vitally, totally, formally, steadily, readily, family.

Neatly, only, firmly, calmly, badly, simply, namely.

Commercial, substantial, circumstantial, beneficial, essential, initial, initials, initialed.

Careful, harmful, grateful, helpful, helpfully, helpfulness.

Dignify, classify, certify, modify, gratified, notified.

Notable, obtainable, pardonable, sensible, horrible, terrible, table, cabled.

READING AND WRITING PRACTICE

63.

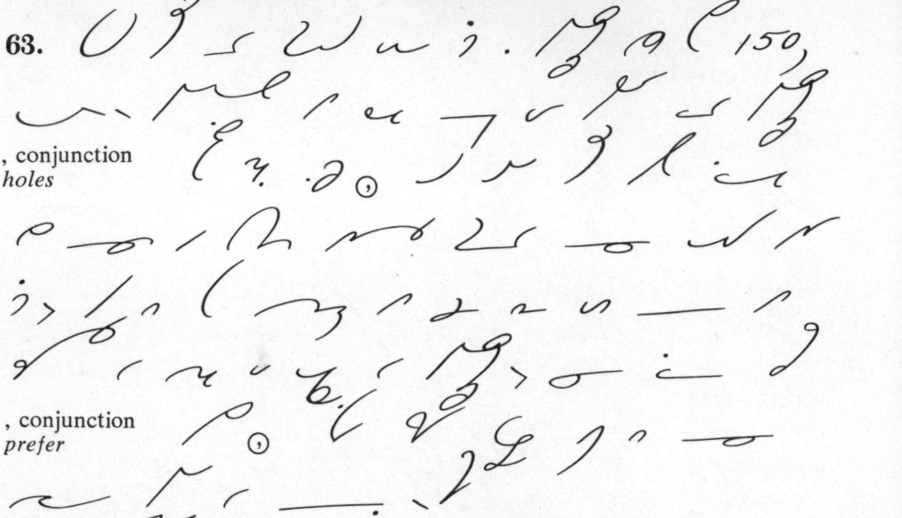

, conjunction
holes

, conjunction
prefer

64.

, *as* clause
requested
, introductory

proceed
, *if* clause

65.

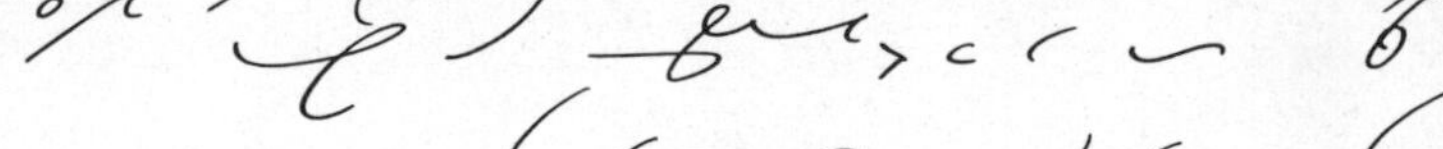

accordance
, introductory

satisfied
, *if* clause

66.

Unless
, introductory

, introductory
dangerous

absorbs
sun's
, parenthetical

, *when* clause
convenience

67. *(shorthand outline)*

, introductory *(shorthand outline)*

ten-year-old
  hyphenated
  before noun *(shorthand outline)*

well built
  no noun,
  no hyphen *(shorthand outline)*

, introductory
acres *(shorthand outline)*

68. *(shorthand outline)*

, conjunction
attention *(shorthand outline)*

expensive
, introductory *(shorthand outline)*

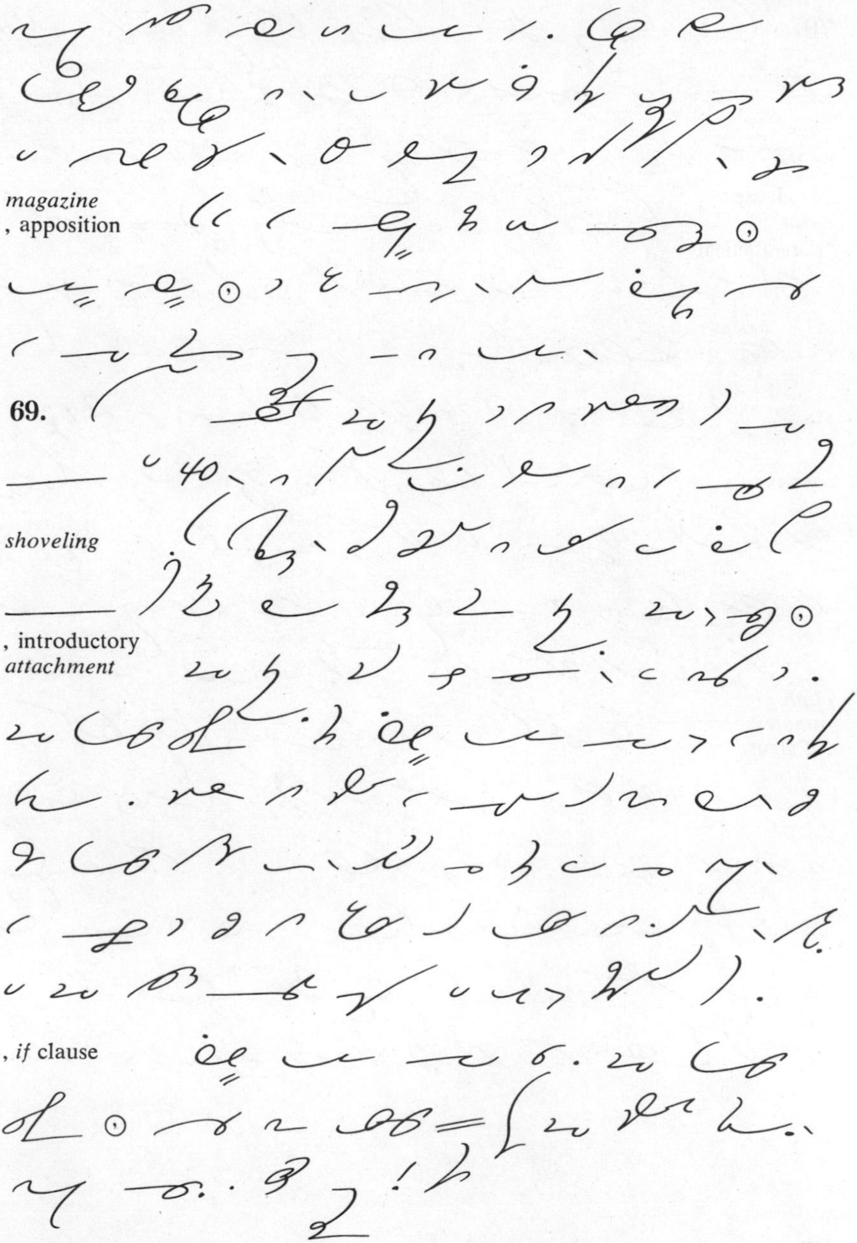

magazine
, apposition

69.

shoveling

, introductory
attachment

, *if* clause

70.

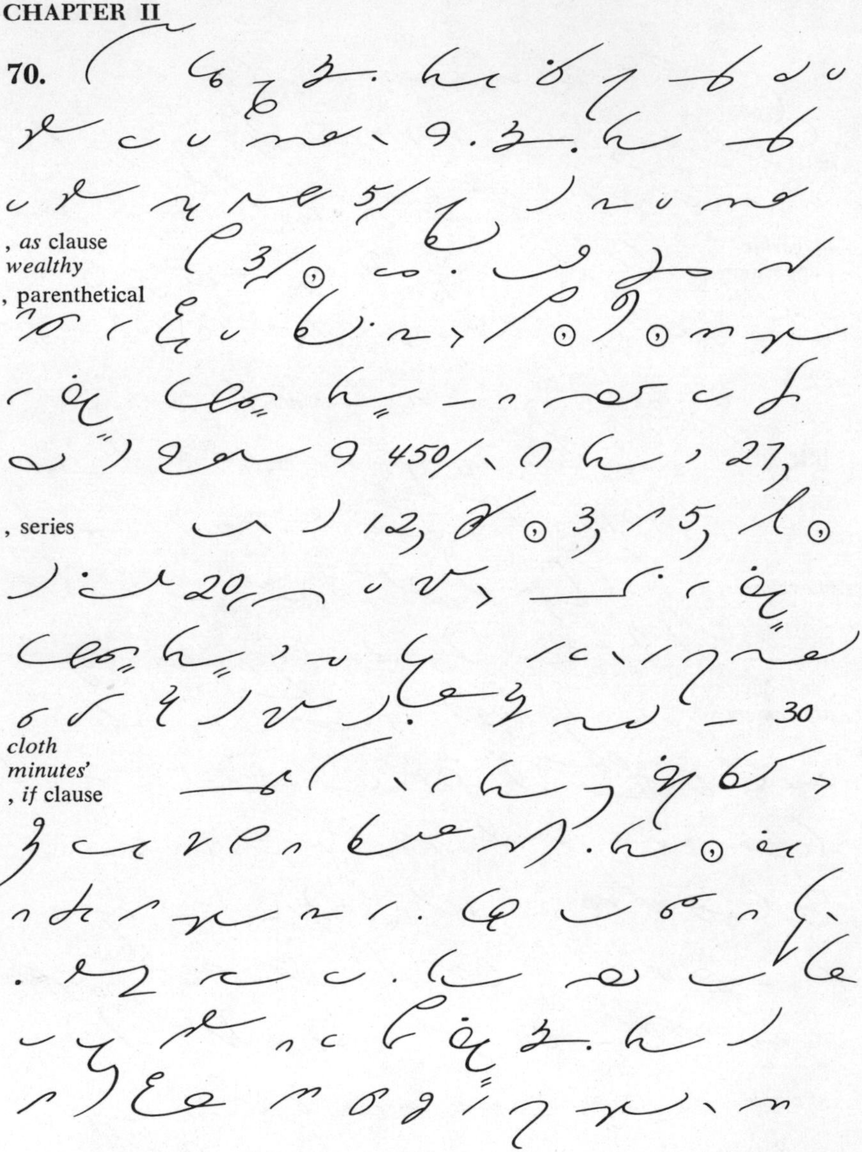

, *as* clause
wealthy
, parenthetical

, series

cloth
minutes'
, *if* clause

LESSON 10

71. WORD-BUILDING PRACTICE—CONSONANTS

NG

NGK

CLOCKWISE TH

COUNTERCLOCKWISE TH

Key
Ring, king, bring, spring, string, sing, hang, sang.
Blank, frank, tank, sank, ink, bank.
These, thick, thickness, thief, thieves, thin, thousand, thus, teeth.
Though, thought, thoughtless, although, threat, thorough, health, wealth.

72. ACCURACY PRACTICE—STRAIGHT LINES

a.

b.

Key
a. It, at; would; did, date; in, not; am, more; men; shall, ship; which.
b. Ate, add, added, any, me, many, may.

CHAPTER II

READING AND WRITING PRACTICE

73. Father Rests

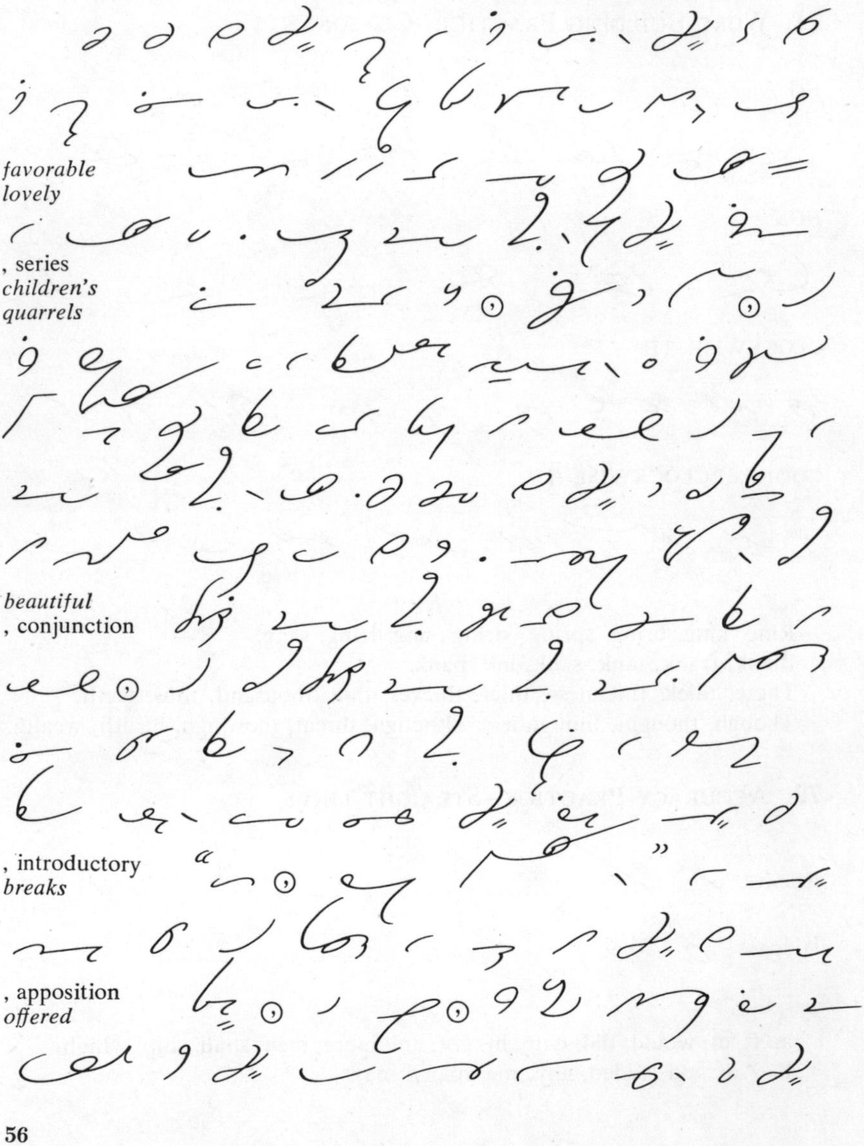

favorable
lovely

, series
children's
quarrels

beautiful
, conjunction

, introductory
breaks

, apposition
offered

, parenthetical
delicate

7:39

, parenthetical
breeze

, introductory
domestic
crisis

permanent
, apposition

current
, introductory

57

CHAPTER II

, conjunction

whatsoever
, introductory

, parenthetical

, introductory
digging

, *as* clause
season
conspire

, *when* clause
, parenthetical
leaves

[Shorthand notations]

, conjunction
bulbs
screens

, *when* clause

Worst
, introductory

, series
cords
leaking
faucets

pane
pitching

, *if* clause

CHAPTER II

disadvantages
adjustment

LESSON 11

74. WORD FAMILIES

-SON

-TIME

-MOST

-VENT

-RATE

Key

Son, reason, unison, person, garrison, comparison, crimson.
Time, noontime, sometime, pastime, daytime, nighttime, lifetime.
Most, foremost, uppermost, utmost, mostly, almost.
Vent, invent, event, convent, prevent, circumvent, advent.
Rate, operate, separate, generate, commemorate, enumerate.

CHAPTER III

75.

, *as* clause
accommodations

, parenthetical
, introductory
capacity

Transcribe:
  January 10
  January 20

76.
five-day
  hyphenated
  before noun
, introductory

man's
sweater
, series

, apposition
past
affection

, *if* clause
maid
occupied

62

77.

, conjunction
hazard
guess

, introductory
leisure

year's
breakfast

employees
, nonrestrictive

mother's
, introductory

24
appetite
develop
, series
, parenthetical

, introducing
    short quote
? inside quote

78.

, parenthetical
family
children

numerous
feasible

two-week
    hyphenated
    before noun

motels
, conjunction

worry
; because of comma
, *when* clause

(shorthand outlines)

, parenthetical
well known
   no noun,
   no hyphen

; illustrative ,

different
, parenthetical

79.

; no conjunction
, introductory

low-cost
   hyphenated
   before noun
, introductory

moderately priced
   no hyphen
   after *ly*
: enumeration
, series

accessible
, conjunction

[Shorthand notes]

, introductory
weekly

inexpensive
facilities
, *and* omitted

Transcribe:
$25

80.

, year date
, introductory

1953

, introductory
, introducing
  short quote
. inside quote

, *if* clause
, courteous
  request

LESSON 12

81. Brief-Form Derivatives

Key

a. Allow, allows, allowed, allowance, allowable, disallow.
b. Stand, standing, stands, understand, withstand, misunderstand.
c. Order, ordering, ordered, orderly, reorder, disorder, disorderly.
d. Progress, progressive, progression, progressed, progresses.
e. Like, likes, likely, likable, dislike.
f. Letter, letters, lettered, lettering, unlettered.

82. Geographical Expressions

Key

a. Washington, Wilmington, Bloomington, Burlington, Bennington.
b. Wisconsin, Michigan, Iowa, Illinois, Indiana, Ohio, Minnesota.
c. France, Spain, Equador, Egypt, Greece, India, Pakistan.

CHAPTER III

READING AND WRITING PRACTICE

83.

Chicago
. inside quote
accessible
travel
attendance
, nonrestrictive
city's
wholehearted
; no conjunction
, *and* omitted
welcome
occasion

84.

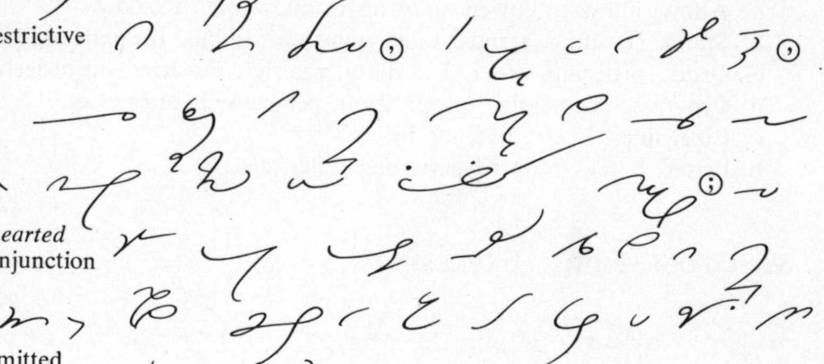

, parenthetical
cordial

usually
maximum
co-operate

85.

pleasure
conversation

, *year date*
, *introductory*

, *and* omitted
recently remodeled
no hyphen
after *ly*

: *enumeration*
, *series*

CHAPTER III

commercial
exhibitors
, parenthetical

reserving
; illustrative ,

furnishings
, *when* clause

separate
self-addressed
distribute

, introductory

, parenthetical
; because of comma
forward

advance
, if clause

86.

acknowledge
forthcoming

exhibit
, if clause
, apposition

; no conjunction
, introductory
available

Black's
, if clause
, as clause

87.

, *as* clause
available

well planned
no noun,
no hyphen
, introductory

Transcribe:
$100

, introductory
telephone

well-known
hyphenated
before noun

LESSON 13

88. USEFUL BUSINESS-LETTER PHRASES

WHICH

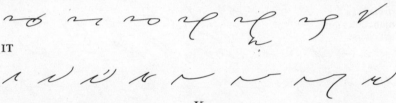

WE

YOU

IT

Key

Which is, which is the, which is not, which means, which you, which you are, which you can, which we are.

We have, we have your letter, we find, we know, we will, we might, we made, we shall.

You might, you must, you may, you may be, you may be sure, you may have, you should.

It is, it is not, it isn't, it is the, it will, it will not, it will not be, it was not.

89. FREQUENT NAMES

a.

b.

Key

a. Clark, Cohen, Cohn, Collins, Connell, Cooper.
b. Beatrice, Belle, Bertha, Bridget, Caroline, Catherine, Celia.

READING AND WRITING PRACTICE

90.

situation
embarrassing
accommodations

courteous
, and omitted

sportsmanlike
, conjunction
, when clause

; illustrative ,
bearing

medium
already
unwittingly

, *as* clause
collector's

, introducing
short quote
. inside quote
91.

souvenirs
, *as* clause

well established
no noun,
no hyphen

, introductory
, parenthetical
unique

CHAPTER III

, parenthetical
correspondence
resort

[shorthand]

welcome
pleasure
; no conjunction

[shorthand]

92.

, introductory
Southern

[shorthand]

12-week
hyphenated
before noun

[shorthand]

engagement
, apposition
; because of comma

[shorthand]

: enumeration

[shorthand]

5:30 8:30

Transcribe:
75 per cent

75,

12

10.

, series
salary

93.

23

accordance
, introductory

12

80 4

19   80   12   20

=Transcribe:
$10
$20

20
10   10

, if clause
definitely

centrally located
no hyphen
  after *ly*
, nonrestrictive

94.

Accordingly
, introductory
, *as* clause

, year date
, apposition
: introducing
  long quote

. inside quote
, introductory
Naturally

LESSON 14

95. Word Beginnings

DE-

DIS-

EM-

EN-

EX-

FORE-

Key

Debate, decision, delinquent, department, deport, designed, depress.
Disarm, discord, discussion, dismayed, displease.
Embarrass, embellish, embezzle, embody, embrace, employ.
Encounter, encourage, endanger, enforcement, engagingly, engrave.
Exceed, exclaim, exclude, excitement, execute, examine.
Foreground, foreman, foremost, forenoon, forestall, forever, foreword.

READING AND WRITING PRACTICE

96. *(shorthand outlines)*

180/

30 *(shorthand outlines)*

, parenthetical
; because of comma
remittance

(shorthand outlines) 30

repeatedly
, conjunction

, introductory
delinquent
various

, conjunction
choice
unless

10

, *if* clause
associations

, introductory
, introducing
short quote
? inside quote

97. *(shorthand outlines)*

Transcribe:
$25
, apposition

five-day
hyphenated
before noun

, nonrestrictive

, parenthetical
, *when* clause
; *no* conjunction

98.

minimum
one-half
banquet

, introductory
well tuned
no noun,
no hyphen

, *if* clause
assistance
arranging

99.
, *as* clause
three-year
    hyphenated
    before noun

, conjunction
, parenthetical

, *and* omitted
irregular
revenue

cities
survey
: enumeration

25

enjoying
equitable
, introductory

100.

activities
semiannual

, introductory
aware
wholehearted

soundproofed
, conjunction

tenure
pleasurable
, series

101.

Speech
, introductory

CHAPTER III

, nonrestrictive
, year date
facilities

1953

, introductory
exhibit

12
organization
, *if* clause
; illustrative ,

exceedingly
assumption

, *if* clause
, introductory

, introducing
  short quote
. inside quote

LESSON 15

102. WORD-BUILDING PRACTICE—BLENDS

-RD

-LD

DET-, DED-

-TED, -DED

MEN, MEM

-XES

Key

Hard, heard, guard, pardon, standard, card, board, toward.
Hold, sold, cold, gold, mold.
Detect, deter, detail, detriment, deduct, deduction.
Rated, parted, hated, debated, needed, graded.
Meant, cement, comment, member, memory.
Fixes, taxes, annexes, relaxes, boxes, mixes, transfixes.

READING AND WRITING PRACTICE

103. Speaking of United States Hotels

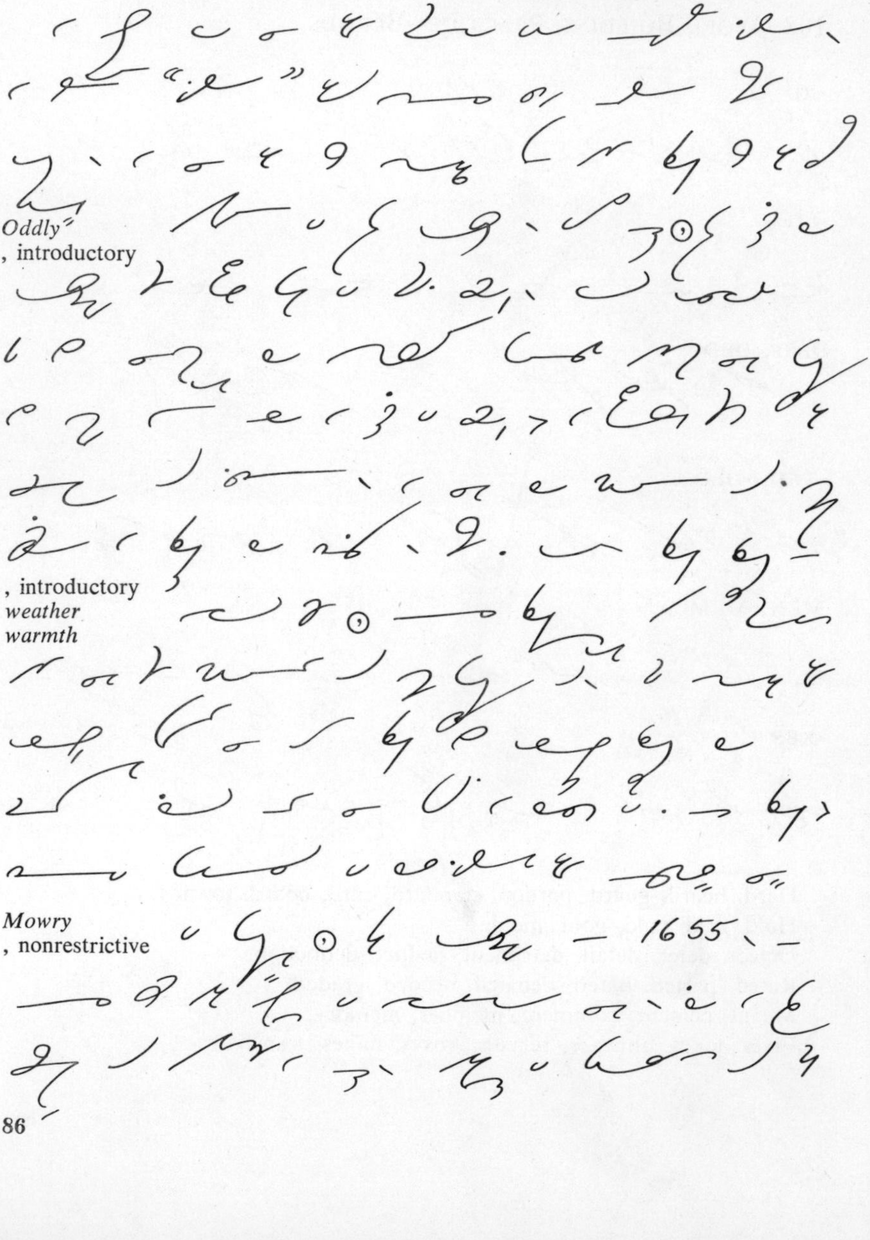

Oddly
, introductory

, introductory
weather
warmth

Mowry
, nonrestrictive

Council
, series

, series
Philadelphia

Fraunces
hotel's
bade

13 ... — 1795

American
; illustrative ,

20=

introductory
summons
promptly

, when clause
, series
families

expansion
, introductory
, series

European
. inside quote
, introductory

1850.

Fifth
, parenthetical   1859   1880

commodious

, series   19

, series
diplomacy
economic

Waldorf-Astoria
; because of comma   (1893-1929)
, apposition

present-day
hyphenated
before noun

CHAPTER III

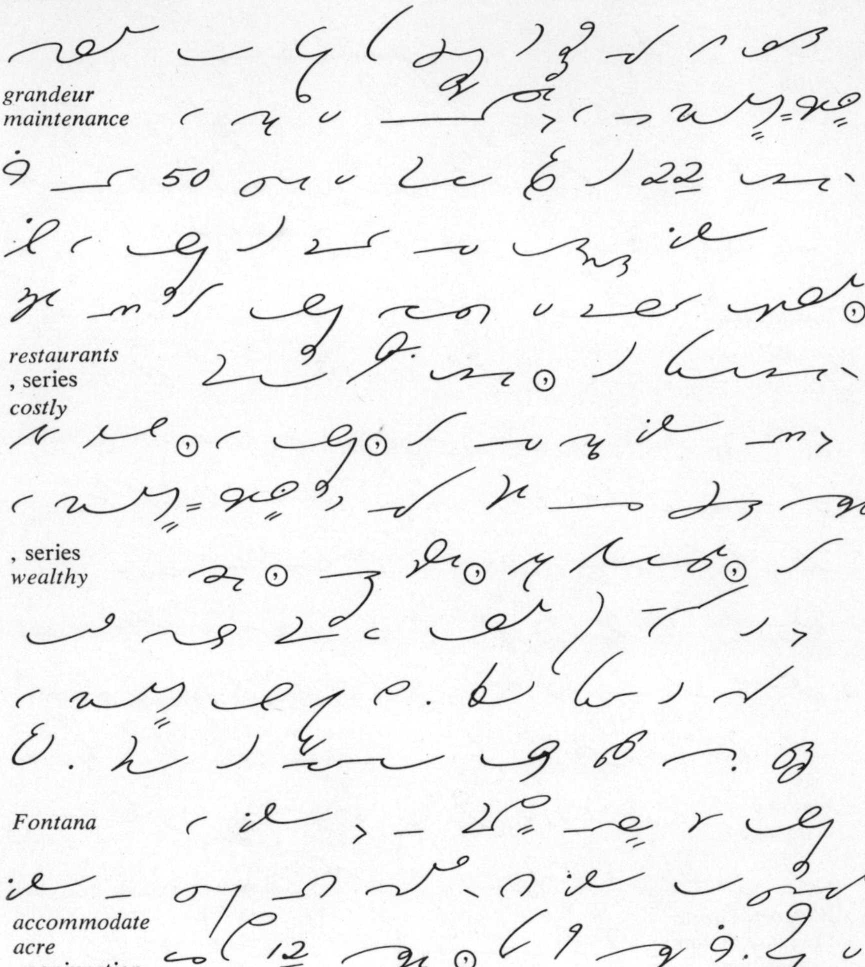

grandeur
maintenance

restaurants
, series
costly

, series
wealthy

Fontana

accommodate
acre
, conjunction

LESSON 16

104. WORD FAMILIES

-WAY

-SCRIBE

-COUNT

-MOUNT

-SIDE

Key

Gateway, roadway, railway, stairway, broadway, doorway.

Transcribe, subscribe, prescribe, describe, inscribe, oversubscribe, circumscribe.

Count, recount, account, miscount, discount, accountant.

Mount, amount, paramount, surmount, dismount.

Inside, beside, roadside, coincide, hillside, preside, countryside.

READING AND WRITING PRACTICE

105.

earnestly
Department's

, *introductory*
; *no conjunction*

, *introductory*
well trained
  no noun,
  no hyphen

, *introductory*
adequate

nationally known
  no hyphen
  after ly

policyholders
, *year date*

106.

, series
; because of comma
, introductory

, parenthetical
, introductory

, introductory

science
advise
, conjunction

, *if* clause
community

107.

, introductory
handling
casualty

CHAPTER IV

; because of comma
, introductory

, introductory
transferred

: enumeration
, series
coverages

, nonrestrictive
equipped

, *and* omitted
; because of comma
, *if* clause

108.

, apposition
previously

[Shorthand notation]

, *when* clause
; no conjunction
, conjunction

109.
: introducing
  long quote
, parenthetical
. inside quote
worry

benefits
disabled
confining

made-to-order
hyphenated
before noun

, introductory

110.

, *if* clause
destroy

; illustrative ,
, series

. courteous
request

LESSON 17

111. BRIEF-FORM DERIVATIVES

Key

a. Wonder, wonders, wondering, wondered, wonderful, wonderfully, wonderingly.

b. Recognize, recognizing, recognized, unrecognized, recognizable, recognition.

c. Enclose, enclosing, encloses, enclosure, enclosures.

d. Remember, remembers, remembered, disremember.

e. Individual, individuals, individually, individualized, individuality, individualist.

f. Business, businesses, businessman, businessmen, businesslike.

112. GEOGRAPHICAL EXPRESSIONS

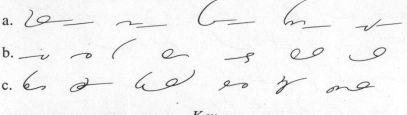

Key

a. Framingham, Cunningham, Birmingham, Buckingham, Nottingham.

b. Missouri, Kentucky, Tennessee, Arkansas, Mississippi, Alabama, Louisiana.

c. Peru, Siam, Poland, Turkey, Sweden, Ukraine.

READING AND WRITING PRACTICE

113.

, if clause
, parenthetical
neighborhood

, parenthetical
effective

, series
accident
agent's

, and omitted
competent

, series
progressive

lifetime
Won't

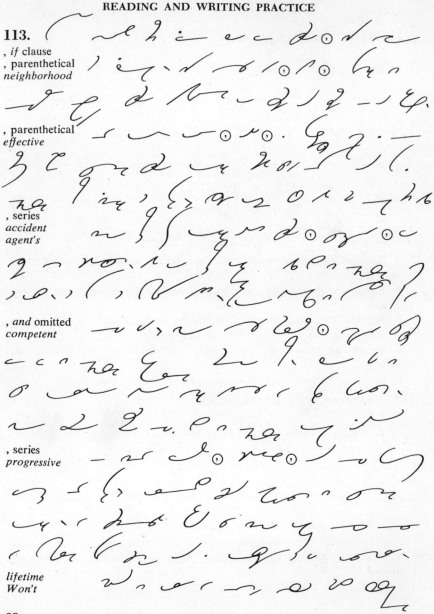

114.

families
, conjunction

up to date
no noun,
no hyphen

, as clause
, series
affect
reviewed

well-trained
hyphenated
before noun

, apposition
Green's

character
ability
, series

115.

, introductory
track

, introductory

, nonrestrictive
local

116.

possessions
; *illustrative* ,
, *series*

representative's
behalf

, *and* omitted
, *when* clause
misfortune

. *courteous*
request

117.

, *series*
children's

, *when* clause
associated

, *introductory*
, *year date*

1915,

, introducing
short quote
. inside quote

118.

companies
year's

, series
unpredictable

past-due
hyphenated
before noun

: enumeration
definite

widely used
no hyphen
after *ly*

LESSON 18

119. USEFUL BUSINESS-LETTER PHRASES

ANY

EACH

FEW

MANY

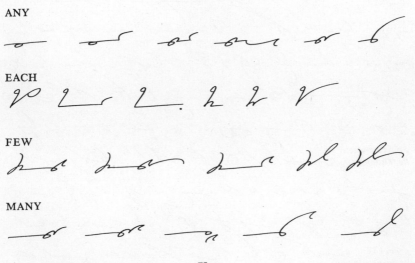

Key

Any more, any more than, any one of the, anyone else, any other, any time.

Each day, each month, each morning, each one, each other, each time.

Few minutes, few minutes ago, few months, few days, few days ago.

Many other, many others, many thousands, many times, many days.

120. FREQUENT NAMES

a.

b.

Key

a. Crowley, Daly, Davidson, Davies, Davis, Donovan, Doyle.
c. Arthur, Benjamin, Charles, Clarence, Daniel, David.

READING AND WRITING PRACTICE

121.

family
adequate

, parenthetical
dependency

proceeds
, conjunction

mother's
, parenthetical

. courteous
request

122.

, parenthetical
partial

involuntary
, *when* clause
destroyed

peak
, introductory

interview
; no conjunction

123.
Transcribe:
    $5,000
, nonrestrictive

, introductory
present-day
    hyphenated
    before noun

evaluating
, *if* clause

determine
, parenthetical

124.

, introductory
motorists

, introductory
, series
enjoyable

, introducing
short quote
accidental

. inside quote
, apposition

: enumeration
safe-and-sane
hyphenated
before noun

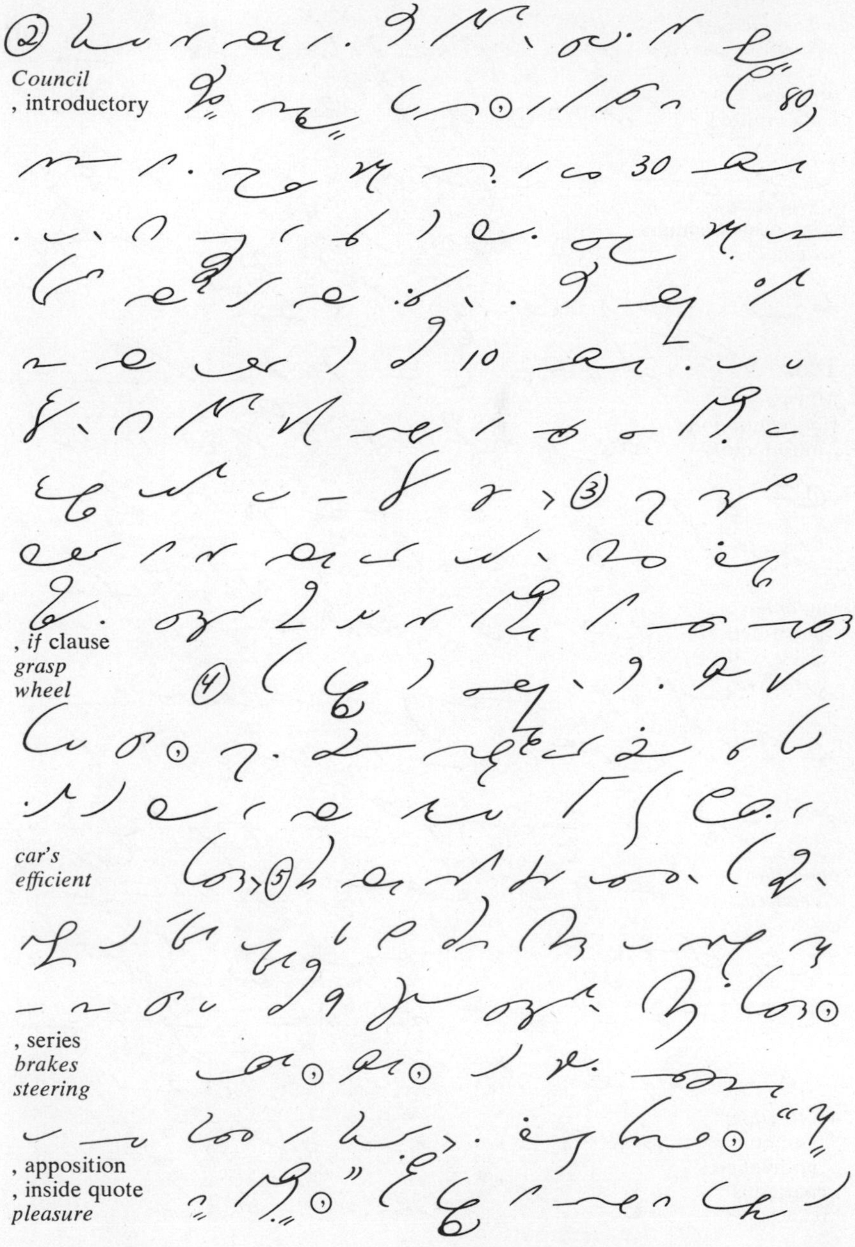

Council
, introductory

, *if* clause
grasp
wheel

car's
efficient

, series
brakes
steering

, apposition
, inside quote
pleasure

CHAPTER IV

practical
, and omitted

, year date
; because of comma
original

125.

Mortgage
Cancellation
, introductory

guarantee
, parenthetical

agreeably
compared

worth while
  no noun,
  no hyphen
. courteous
  request

LESSON 19

126. WORD ENDINGS

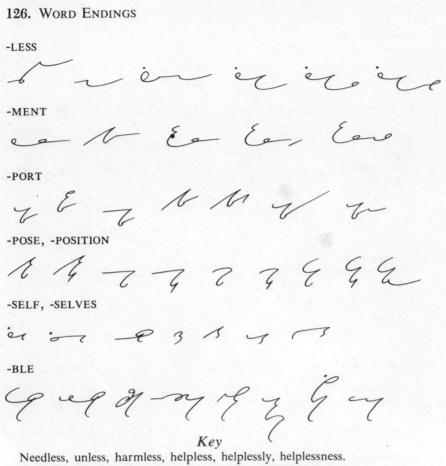

-LESS

-MENT

-PORT

-POSE, -POSITION

-SELF, -SELVES

-BLE

Key

Needless, unless, harmless, helpless, helplessly, helplessness.

Element, department, supplement, supplemented, supplementary.

Report, export, import, deport, deportation, reported, reporter.

Dispose, disposition, impose, imposition, compose, composition, propose, proposition, proposal.

Herself, himself, myself, yourself, itself, ourselves, themselves.

Pliable, reliable, excitable, incurable, traceable, respectable, habitable, honorable.

CHAPTER IV

READING AND WRITING PRACTICE

127.

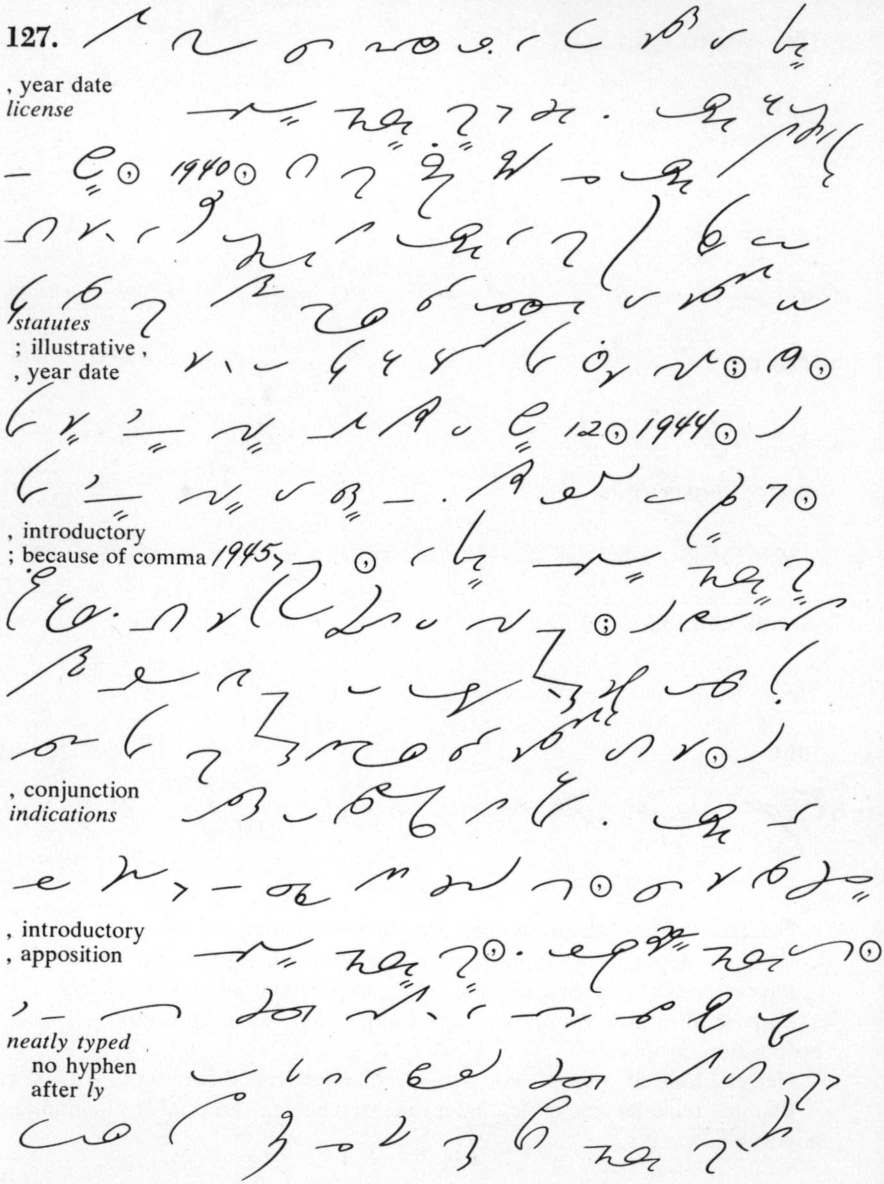

, year date
license

statutes
; illustrative ,
, year date

, introductory
; because of comma

, conjunction
indications

, introductory
, apposition

neatly typed
no hyphen
after *ly*

128.

, *as* clause
year-by-year
  hyphenated
  before noun

nation's
, *and* omitted
, parenthetical

renewal
, nonrestrictive

, introductory

129.

film
, parenthetical

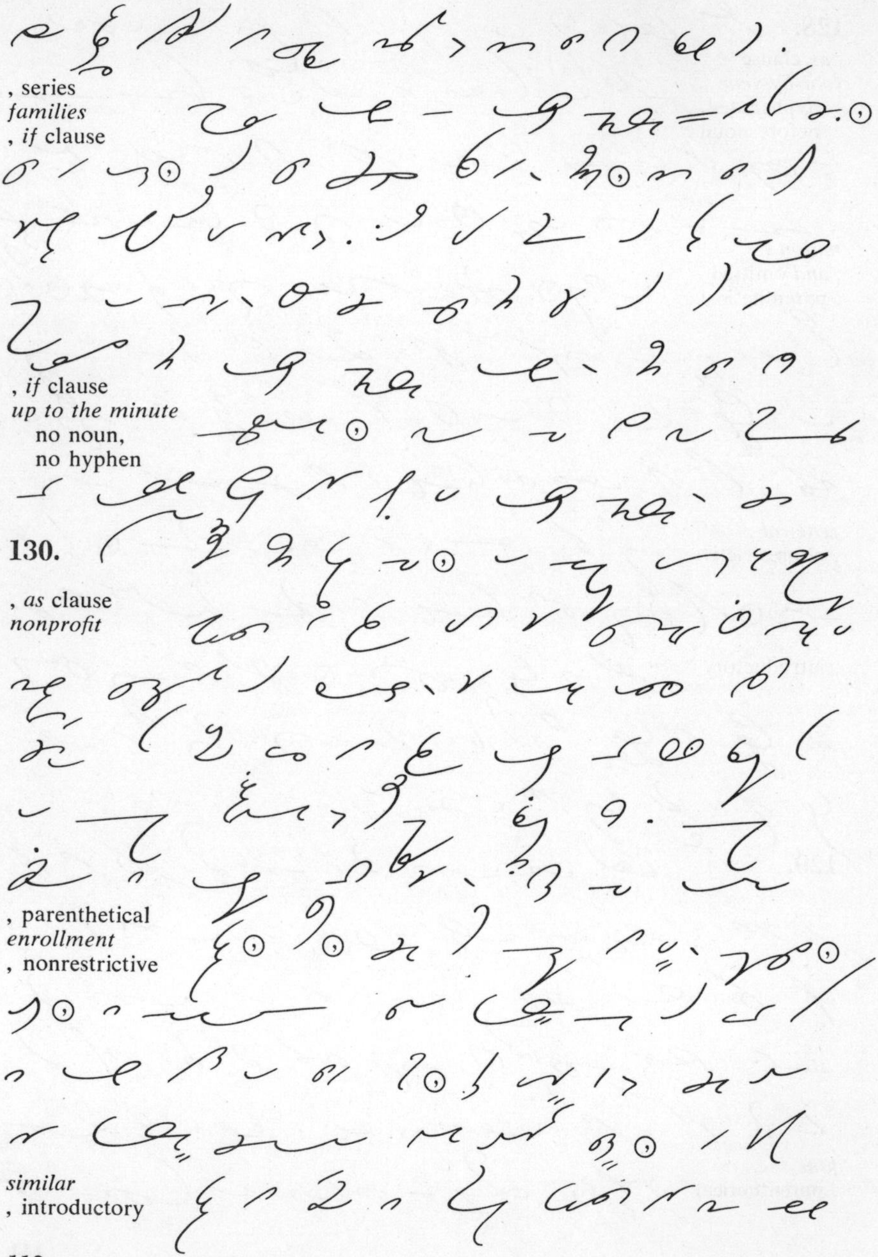

, series
families
, *if* clause

, *if* clause
up to the minute
no noun,
no hyphen

130.

, *as* clause
nonprofit

, parenthetical
enrollment
, nonrestrictive

similar
, introductory

[Shorthand outlines]

, introductory
area

, *if* clause

pleasure
, conjunction

131.
, *as* clause
affecting
occurred
, introductory

, introductory

, introductory
, parenthetical
substantiate

132.
, introducing short quote
. inside quote
, introductory
, parenthetical

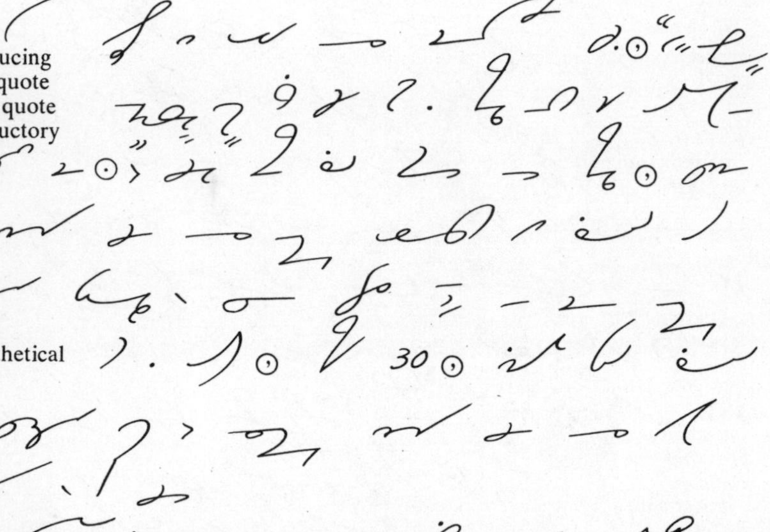

133.
happiness
derives
, *when* clause

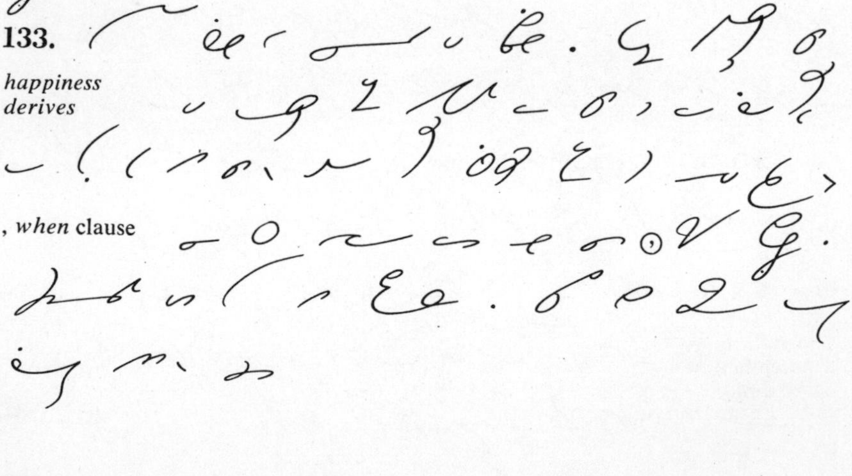

LESSON 20

134. WORD-BUILDING PRACTICE—OMISSION OF VOWELS

OMISSION OF SHORT U

OMISSION OF OW

OMISSION OF E IN DIPHTHONG U

OMISSION OF MINOR VOWEL

Key
Some summer, come, become, begun, run, fun.
Count, account, accountant, discount, noun, pronoun, renounce, denounce.
New, renew, renewal, menu, manuscript, neutral.
Theory, genius, companion, envious, previous, serious, tedious, various.

135. ACCURACY PRACTICE—CIRCLES

a.

b.

Key
a. Air, ail, ache, ago, gay, return, rate.
b. Lead, take, tag, teeth, detain.

READING AND WRITING PRACTICE

136. Why Does A Man Buy Life Insurance?

, parenthetical
discussion

vowed
, parenthetical

pronounced
, introducing
short quote
. inside quote

, apposition
dawn

[shorthand outlines]

reassure
deceased
wholly

, introductory
, parenthetical

, *and* omitted

; no conjunction
honored
recipient

137. Ordinary Life Insurance

conceivable
stake

, introductory
grown
children's

, introductory

promptly
prearranged
liquidation

, *as* clause
different

[shorthand]

, series
semiannually
quarterly

[shorthand]

138. Industrial Life Insurance

[shorthand] 1854.

, and omitted
frequent

[shorthand]

societies
growth

[shorthand] 1875

[shorthand]

, introductory
weekly

, nonrestrictive

139. Group Life Insurance

; because of comma
, as clause

, introductory
medical

employee

year's

—*Handbook of Life Insurance*
Institute of Life Insurance

LESSON 21

140. WORD FAMILIES

-ER

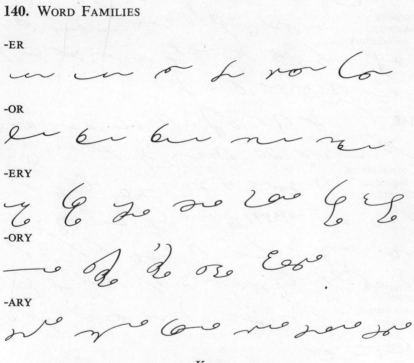

-OR

-ERY

-ORY

-ARY

Key

Rocker, locker, thicker, picker, striker, blacker.

Tailor, sailor, parlor, color, councilor.

Robbery, bribery, refinery, cannery, flattery, bravery, slavery.

Memory, advisory, supervisory, accessory, explanatory.

Secondary, customary, primary, contrary, secretary, sanitary.

CHAPTER V

READING AND WRITING PRACTICE

141.
Transcribe:
$50
, introductory

canceled
exists
, introductory

142.

, parenthetical
, apposition
deceased

proceeds
. courteous
request

143.

, parenthetical
, year date
until

, *when* clause
; because of comma
balances
, introductory
, series
dependable
worth while
no noun,
no hyphen

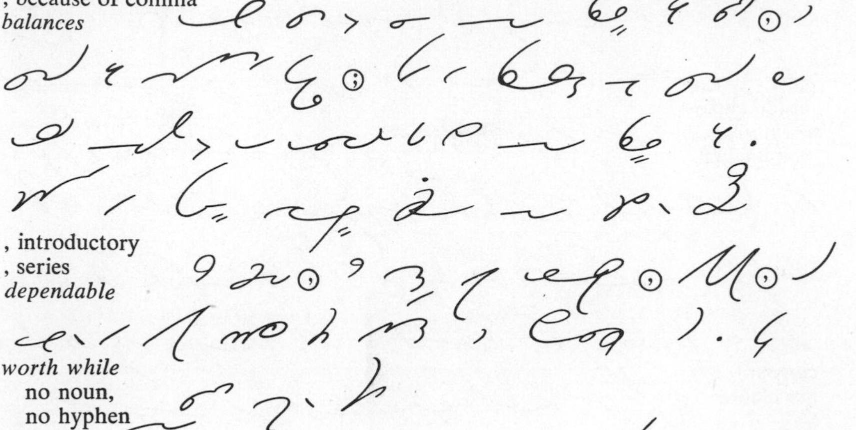

144.

, introductory
pleasant
, *and* omitted
, *if* clause
reopen

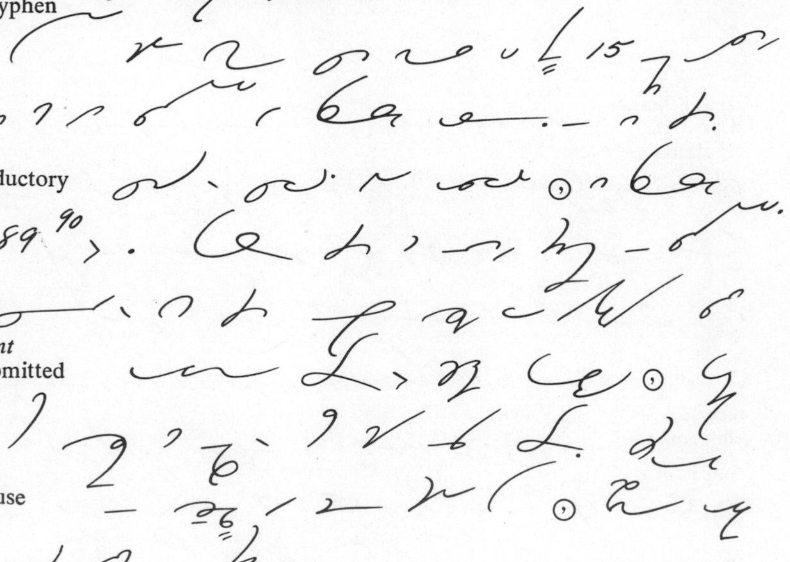

145.

lien
referred

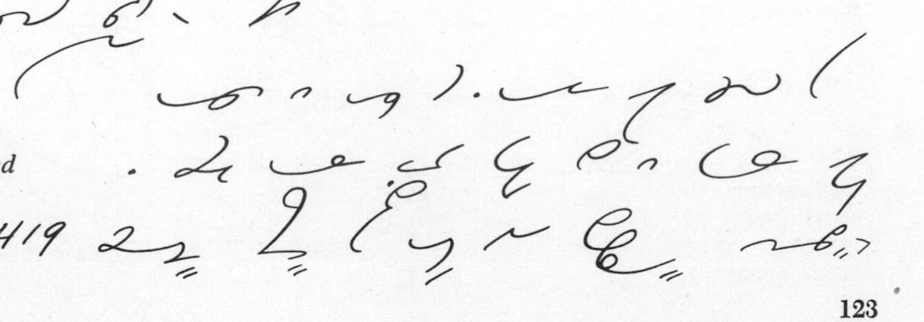

, introducing
  short quote

. inside quote
recommended
, conjunction

146.

current
, *as* clause

, parenthetical
immediate
, *if* clause

necessity
, introductory

, parenthetical

147.
, introducing
  short quote
, introductory
  inside quote

124

; illustrative ,
fulfilled
requirements

, *and* omitted
unsecured

, nonrestrictive
accountant
accepted

; no conjunction
, introductory
believe

148.

insufficient
, *when* clause
inside quote

, introductory
procedure

149.
inability
sufficient
, *as* clause

partner's
resources
, introductory

advise
financial

LESSON 22

150. Brief-Form Derivatives

a.
b.
c.
d.
e.
f.

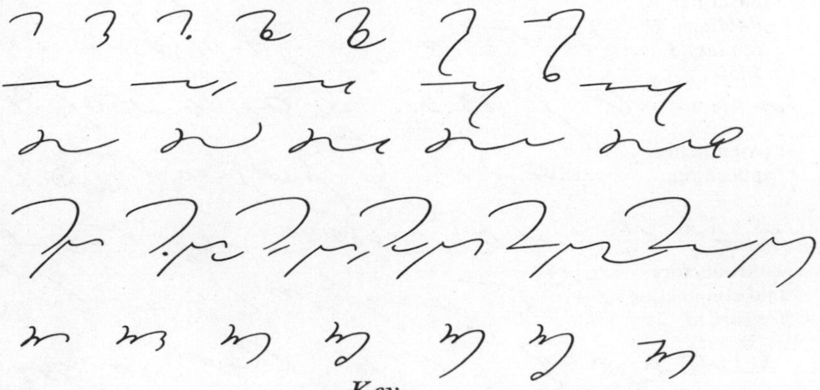

Key

a. Question, questions, questioning, questioner, questionnaire, questionable, unquestionably.

b. Market, marketed, markets, marketable, unmarketable.

c. Circle, circled, circles, circular, circularize.

d. Govern, governing, governed, governor, government, governmental.

e. Direct, director, directed, direction, directional, directive.

f. Success, successes, successful, successfully, successive, successively, unsuccessful.

151. Geographical Expressions

a.
b.
c.

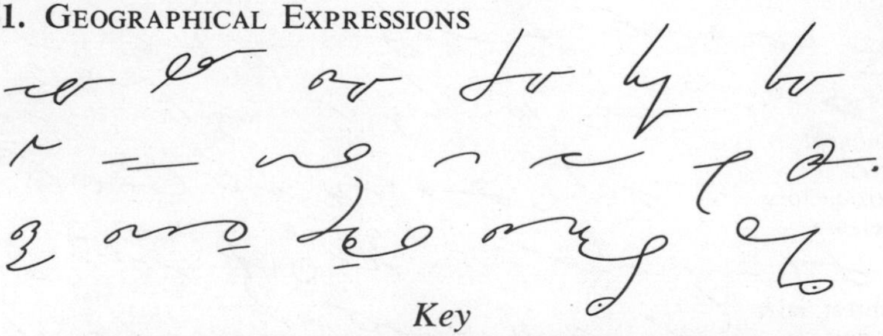

Key

a. Norristown, Tarrytown, Youngstown, Jamestown, Georgetown, Johnstown.

b. Texas, New Mexico, Oklahoma, Kansas, Colorado, Nebraska, Wyoming.

c. U.S.S.R. Uruguay, Venezuela, Yugoslavia, Albania.

READING AND WRITING PRACTICE

152.
Transcribe:
February 28
January 1
$250

(shorthand outlines) 28

(shorthand outlines) 23

(shorthand outlines) 250

, parenthetical
, apposition

(shorthand outlines) 27

, introductory
; no conjunction
forwarded

(shorthand outlines) 480

153.

(shorthand outlines) 29

received
, *if* clause

(shorthand outlines) 40

delinquent
carried
, introductory
, *if* clause

(shorthand outlines) 10

, nonrestrictive
past due
no noun,
no hyphen

154.

Transcribe:
No. 49783

, *as* clause
drawn

, *when* clause
; no conjunction

155.

energy
, series

, nonrestrictive
, year date

National's

: introducing
long quote
ragged

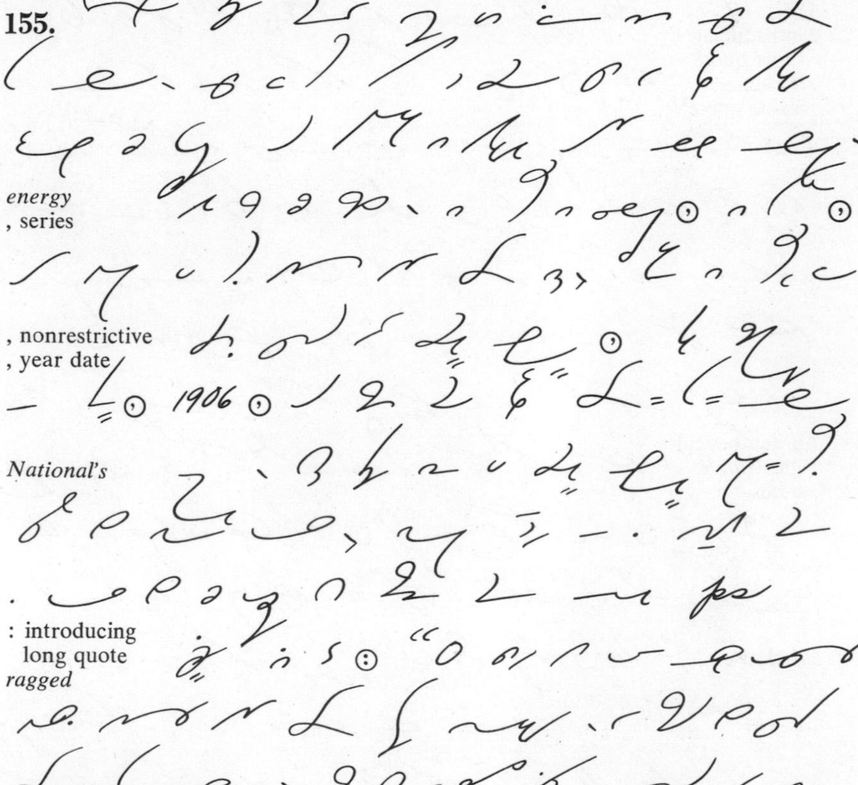

, *as* clause

, *when* clause
receipt

. inside quote
. courteous
  request

156.
, introducing
  short quote
, *if* clause
  inside quote

, parenthetical
; illustrative ,
, series

, *if* clause

, series
; because of comma
resources

Thanksgiving
, conjunction

, *if* clause
library

157.

, introductory

? *well spent*
no noun,
no hyphen

, introductory
, series

158.

, introductory
safeguard
, series

, *and* omitted
well-trained
  hyphenated
  before noun

intelligent
, series

, *when* clause
won't

LESSON 23

159. USEFUL BUSINESS-LETTER PHRASES

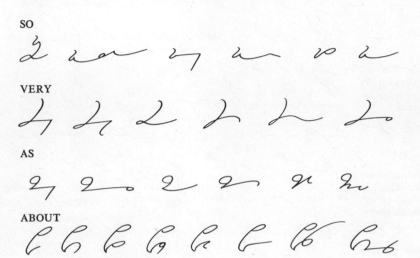

SO

VERY

AS

ABOUT

Key

So far, so little, so much, so long, so that, so well.

Very much, very important, very well, very good, very glad, very many.

As much, as many, as well, as good, as it is, as you know.

About the, about this, about that, about these, about those, about them, about that time, about this matter.

160. FREQUENT NAMES

a.

b.

Key

a. Driscoll, Duffy, Duncan, Dunne, Edwards, Evans, Farrell.

b. Charlotte, Clara, Constance, Cora, Cynthia, Delia.

READING AND WRITING PRACTICE

161.

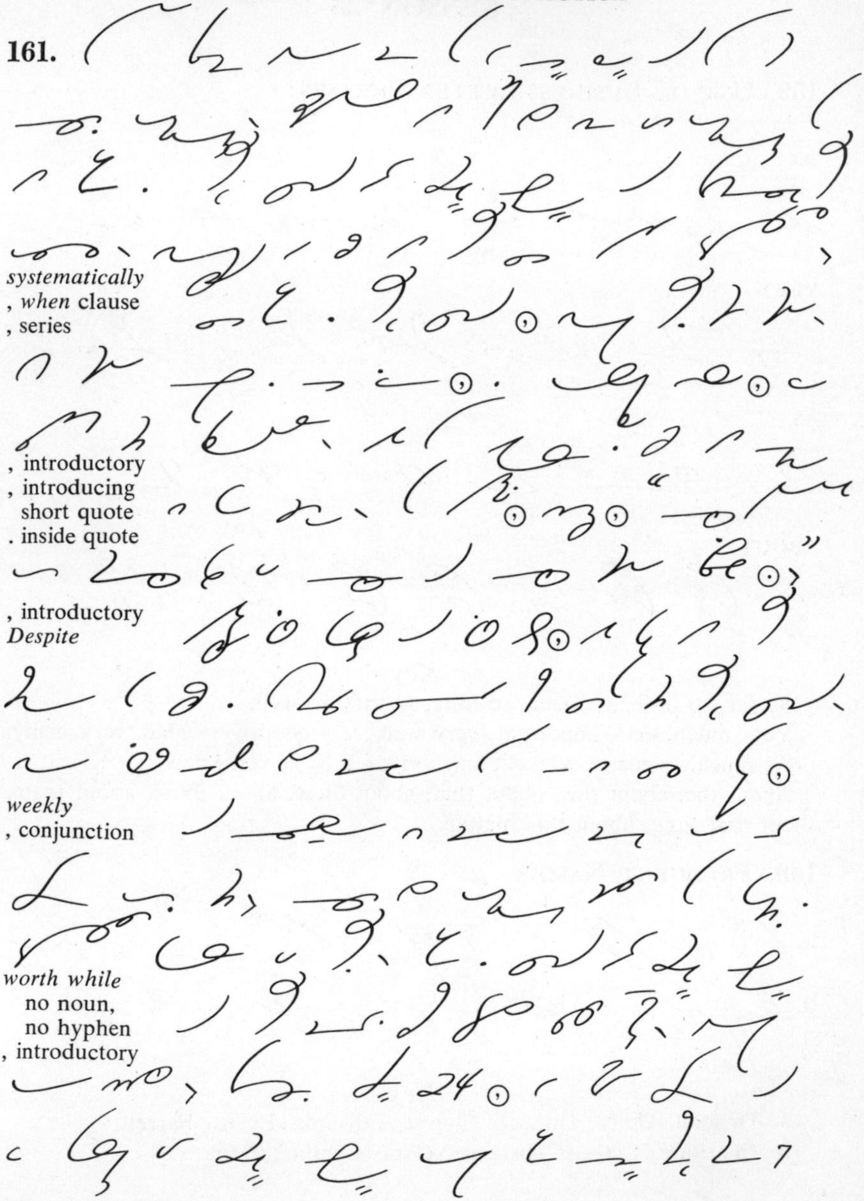
systematically
, *when* clause
, series
, introductory
, introducing short quote
. inside quote
, introductory
Despite
weekly
, conjunction
worth while
no noun, no hyphen
, introductory

rapidly growing
no hyphen
after *ly*

162.

, introductory
low-cost
hyphenated
before noun

yours
: enumeration

, *and* omitted
flexible
, *if* clause

; no conjunction
beginning

, *if* clause
maturity

depositor
, series

financial
. courteous
 request

163.

, *as* clause
, series

exhibit
appliances
, *when* clause

electrical
, *if* clause

, introducing
 short quote
. inside quote
, *when* clause

; because of comma
; no conjunction

, introductory

164.

, *when* clause
   inside quote

, *if* clause
, introductory
; illustrative ,

, series
, *when* clause
cosigners

worth-while
   hyphenated
   before noun

. courteous
  request
, introductory

165.

, *as* clause
readily
severe

badly needed
no hyphen
after *ly*
, series

, *if* clause
, nonrestrictive

166.

, year date
Transcribe:
$40,000

, parenthetical
resources
area

, parenthetical
Bedford's

LESSON 24

167. Word Beginnings

IM-

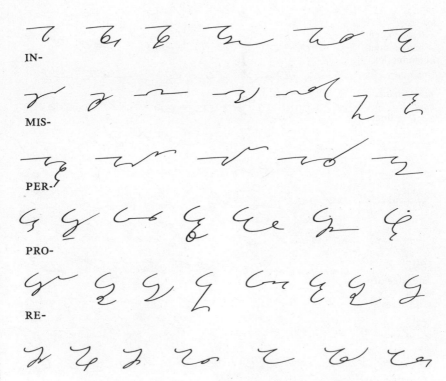

IN-

MIS-

PER-

PRO-

RE-

Key

Impose, impartial, impatient, impersonal, impolite, improper.

Incident, incite, income, inconsistent, incredible, injure, inspect.

Misconception, misconduct, misdirect, misguided, misinform.

Persist, persuade, permit, perspire, perplex, perfume, perhaps.

Procedure, professor, profound, project, pronounce, prosper, professional, profane.

Refute, refresh, refuse, reflect, repel, reprint, replenish.

READING AND WRITING PRACTICE

168. *[shorthand outlines]*

low-cost
   hyphenated
   before noun
, conjunction

maintenance
canceled
, and omitted

manager
, apposition

169.
, introductory
worry
possessions

, parenthetical
Transcribe:
   20 per cent

: enumeration
, series
policies

, introductory

, *when* clause
receive

, introductory
identify

tomorrow
, apposition

170.

, introductory
, series

, introductory
, *when* clause
attendant

, introductory

, introductory
maximum
occasion

, nonrestrictive
, year date

1898

171.

, series
, introductory

Whether
, introductory

: introducing
long quote

, *if* clause
. inside quote
, *when* clause

[shorthand]

Transcribe:
75 cents
$100

[shorthand]

172. *[shorthand]*

, introductory
survey

[shorthand]

; because of comma
, *if* clause

[shorthand]

, conjunction
convenience

[shorthand]

, *when* clause
, parenthetical

[shorthand]

effect
heirs
exceedingly

173.

, conjunction

cashiers'
, series
, *if* clause

, *when* clause

, parenthetical
theft

misfortune
; no conjunction

LESSON 25

174. WORD-BUILDING PRACTICE—BLENDS

NT

MD

GENT, PEND

TIVE

TEN

TEM

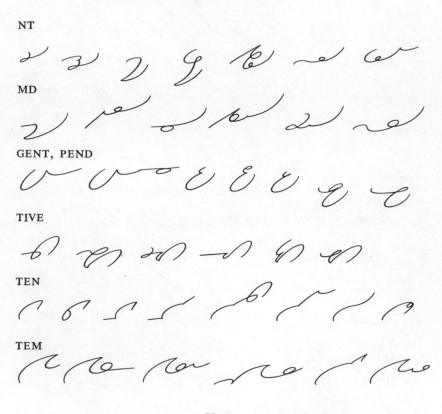

Key

Sent, consent, convent, prevent, disappoint, current, printer.
Informed, dreamed, named, disarmed, farmed, claimed.
Gentle, gentleman, spend, expend, opened, ripened, legend.
Native, captive, sensitive, motive, positive, restive.
Tension, attention, intention, intent, tentative, tender, tenant, tennis.
Temper, temperament, temperature, contemplate, temptation, temporary.

READING AND WRITING PRACTICE

175. The Typewriter

equality
barriers
servitude

domestic
factory
revolution

, *introductory*

operate
. *inside quote*
, *conjunction*

. *inside quote*
Unthinkable
, *introductory*

male
heretofore
laboriously

engineer
practical
device

blank-book
  hyphenated
  before noun

Glidden
Soule
Sholes
, series

, nonrestrictive
appeared

1714

1867

CHAPTER V

[Shorthand notation — not transcribable as text]

earmarks
sewing
; illustrative ,

Densmore
, apposition

, *when* clause
promptly

, apposition

, introductory
Transcribe:
No. 1

6 — 1874,

; no conjunction
, introductory
steel

125/-

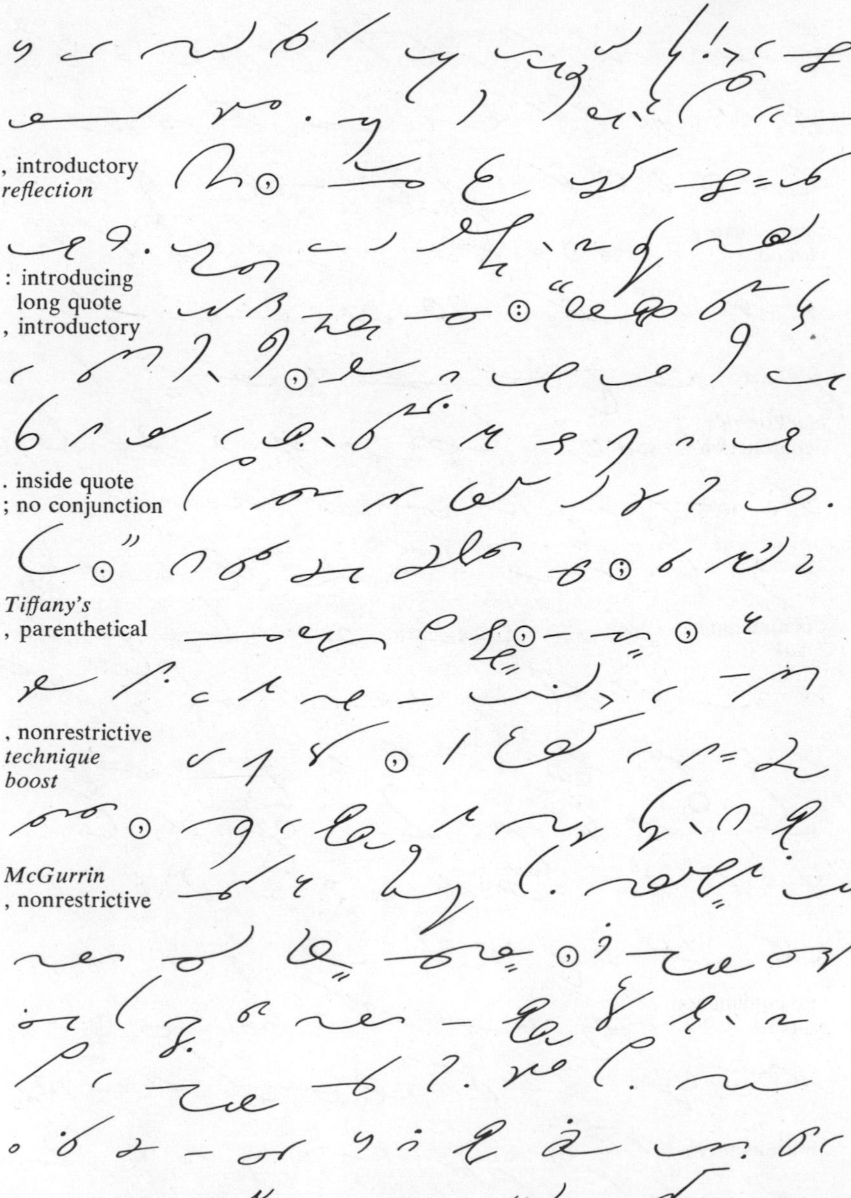
, introductory
reflection
: introducing long quote
, introductory
. inside quote
; no conjunction
Tiffany's
, parenthetical
, nonrestrictive
technique
boost
McGurrin
, nonrestrictive
; no conjunction

CHAPTER V

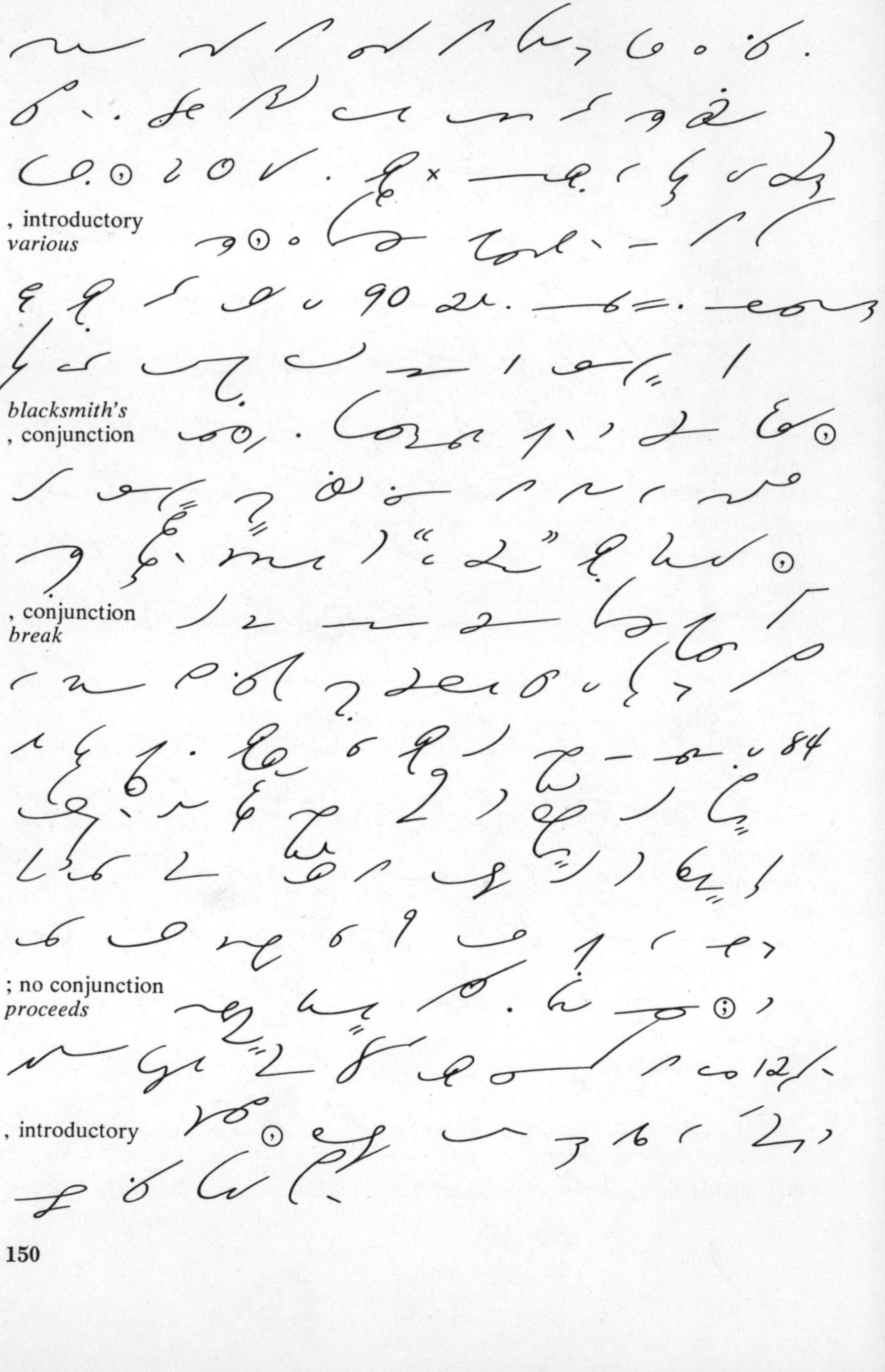

, introductory
various

blacksmith's
, conjunction

, conjunction
break

; no conjunction
proceeds

, introductory

LESSON 26

176. WORD FAMILIES

-ISH

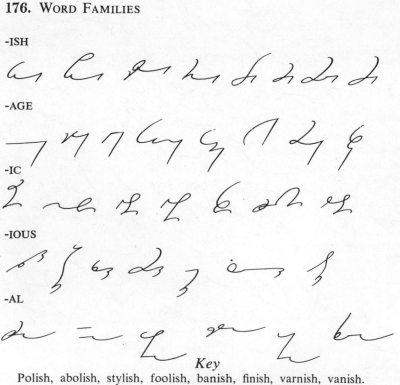

-AGE

-IC

-IOUS

-AL

Key

Polish, abolish, stylish, foolish, banish, finish, varnish, vanish.

Manage, storage, tonnage, brokerage, personage, damage, village, passage.

Civic, classic, traffic, tragic, basic, scientific, terrific.

Tedious, obvious, serious, various, envious, harmonious, devious.

Final, internal, original, external, regional, journal.

CHAPTER VI

READING AND WRITING PRACTICE

177.
screeching
brakes
scream

, conjunction
accidents

: enumeration
maximum

, year date
; because of comma
tragic

, introductory
leaflet

, apposition
. courteous
  request

178.

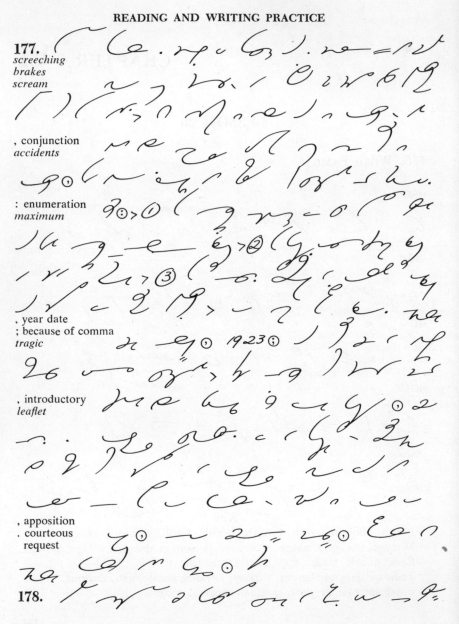

, parenthetical
manufactured

[shorthand notes]

, conjunction

[shorthand notes]

, series
skidding

[shorthand notes]

, apposition

[shorthand notes]

, nonrestrictive

179.

[shorthand notes]

, series
weeks'

[shorthand notes]

, *when* clause
gamble

, introductory
assurance

Transcribe:
  82 per cent
  currently

, *if* clause

180.
; because of comma
, introductory
stadium

, parenthetical
cloud

, introductory
performance

; no conjunction
, *and* omitted
unsurpassed

smartly styled
no hyphen
after *ly*

, series
amazing

, introductory
, introducing
short quote
. inside quote

181.

, apposition
ten-page
hyphenated
before noun
∪ . 10 = 6

; because of comma
, introductory
criticize
draft

CHAPTER VI

(shorthand outlines)

; illustrative ,
, series
  inside quote
. inside quote

(shorthand outlines)

worth while
  no noun,
  no hyphen

(shorthand outlines)

, *as* clause
manuscript
criticisms

182.
, conjunction
critically
margins

(shorthand outlines)

, parenthetical
color

(shorthand outlines)

LESSON 27

183. BRIEF-FORM DERIVATIVES

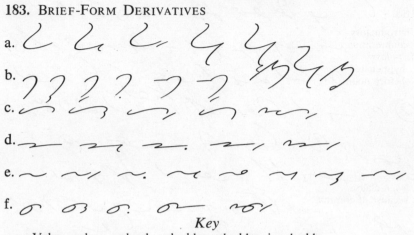

Key

a. Value, values, valued, valuable, valuables, invaluable.

b. Cover, covers, covered, covering, uncover, uncovered, discover, discovery.

c. Organize, organizes, organized, organization, unorganized.

d. Number, numbers, numbering, numbered, unnumbered.

e. Correct, corrected, correcting, corrects, correctly, correction, corrections, uncorrected.

f. Acknowledge, acknowledges, acknowledging, acknowledgment, unacknowledged.

184. GEOGRAPHICAL EXPRESSIONS

Key

a. Evanston, Cranston, Charleston, Galveston, Brockton.

b. Nebraska, South Dakota, North Dakota, Montana, Idaho, Washington, Oregon.

c. Austria, Bulgaria, Finland, Germany, Hungary.

CHAPTER VI

READING AND WRITING PRACTICE

185.

, introductory
: enumeration
first-class
hyphenated
before noun
, *when* clause
; because of comma
well trained
no noun,
no hyphen

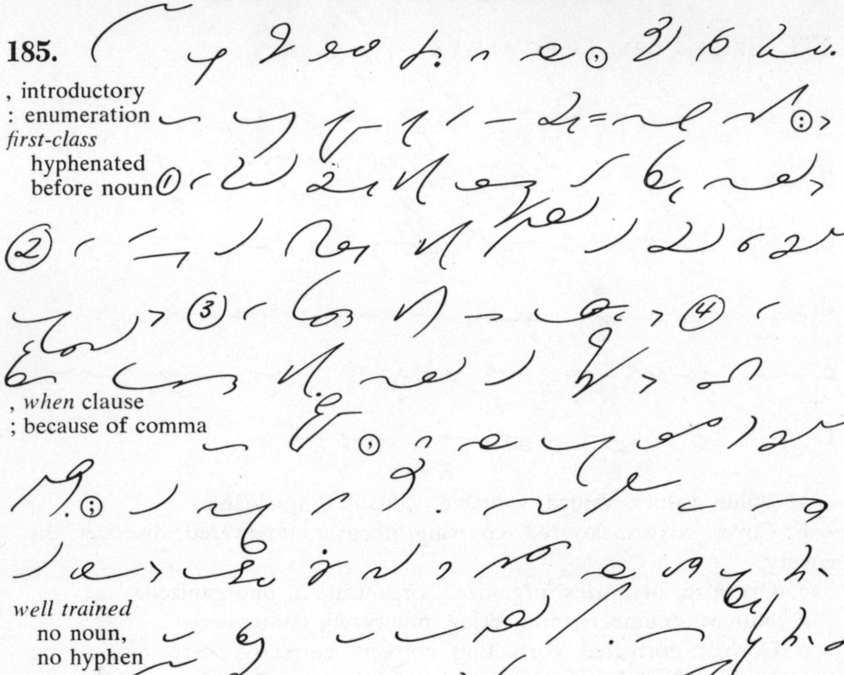

186.

, introductory
modern
, introductory

acquainted
, nonrestrictive

187.

Transcribe:
$250

source
revenue
develop

, introducing
short quote
? inside quote

agent's
license

; illustrative ,
, series

, if clause
discrepancies
immediately

deposit
, when clause

188. [shorthand] 15 ⊙ 1952 ⊙ ○ [shorthand]

, year date

30 ⊙ 1953
, introductory
Vehicle
canceled
, if clause

189.

, introductory

*forwarding
territory*
, nonrestrictive

, introductory
, parenthetical

. courteous
request
, *if* clause

190.

, *and* omitted
; no conjunction
, introductory

191.

Unfortunately
, parenthetical

; because of comma
unlikely

, conjunction
Transcribe:
  40 per cent

, *if clause*

; because of comma
, *if clause*

192.

, introductory
responsibility

, introductory
, conjunction
functioning

LESSON 28

193. USEFUL BUSINESS-LETTER PHRASES

FROM

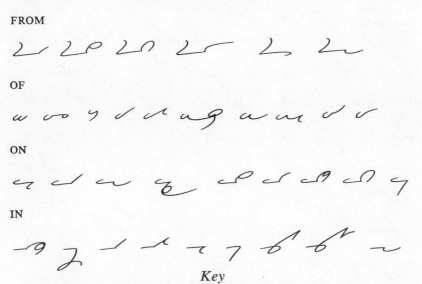

OF

ON

IN

Key

From it, from that, from this, from them, from you, from our.
Of all, of any, of his, of it, of its, of life, of our, of ours, of their, of the.
On his, on it, on our, on sale, on that, on the, on these, on this, on which.
In case, in fact, in it, in its, in his, in which, in addition, in addition to the, in our.

194. FREQUENT NAMES

a.
b.

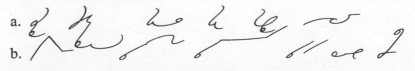

Key

a. Fisher, Fitzgerald, Foley, Fox, Fraser, Gordon.
b. Duncan, Edgar, Edmond, Edward, Ernest, Eugene.

163

READING AND WRITING PRACTICE

195.

Principals
: introducing
  long quote

. inside quote

, parenthetical
families

*equip
inexperienced*
, *and* omitted

, parenthetical
quality

, *if* clause
curriculum

describing
; illustrative ,

badly needed
no hyphen
after ly

196.
, introductory
courses

, introductory
financial

faculty
, when clause

197.
, year date
; because of comma
truly

1953

, apposition

manager

198.
, parenthetical
acquaintances

, if clause

199.
year's
, nonrestrictive
inside quote

brand-new
hyphenated
before noun

200.

; no conjunction
appreciate

performance
permanent

201.

, apposition
February

, if clause
garage

accept
success
happiness

, when clause

202.

suggested
, as clause

Transcribe:
$45
, apposition

4-3211

LESSON 29

203. WORD ENDINGS

-TION

-SUME, -SUMPTION

-TERN, -TERM

-THER

-UAL

-TURE

Key

Mention, action, fashion, detention, prevention, nation, national, nationally.

Resume, presume, assume, consume, consumer, resumption, assumption.

Stern, lantern, attorney, fraternal, eternal, determine.

Mother, brother, father, bother, other, gather, gathered.

Annual, manual, manually, gradual, schedule.

Nature, creature, feature, mature, matured, immature.

READING AND WRITING PRACTICE

204.

[shorthand outlines]

eligible
: enumeration
, series

[shorthand outlines]

enhance
prestige
instill

[shorthand outlines]

recommend
enclosed

[shorthand outlines]

205.

license
, *when* clause

[shorthand outlines]

, conjunction

, year date
; because of comma
, apposition
wife's

, introductory
title

206.

, *as* clause
notarized

H-82774

; because of comma
, parenthetical
appeared

, *if* clause
assistance

207.

co-operation
dealers'
submitting

, conjunction
numerous

, parenthetical
. courteous
   request

up to date
   no noun,
   no hyphen

208.

, series
scientifically
grime

, series
, introductory

appearances
, introductory

, series

, introducing
   short quote
, *and* omitted
. inside quote

month's
, *if* clause

millions

209.
Brook's
parenthetical

, introductory
premium

customer's
presence

; illustrative ,

210.

advised
, introductory

, apposition
, introductory
employment

211.

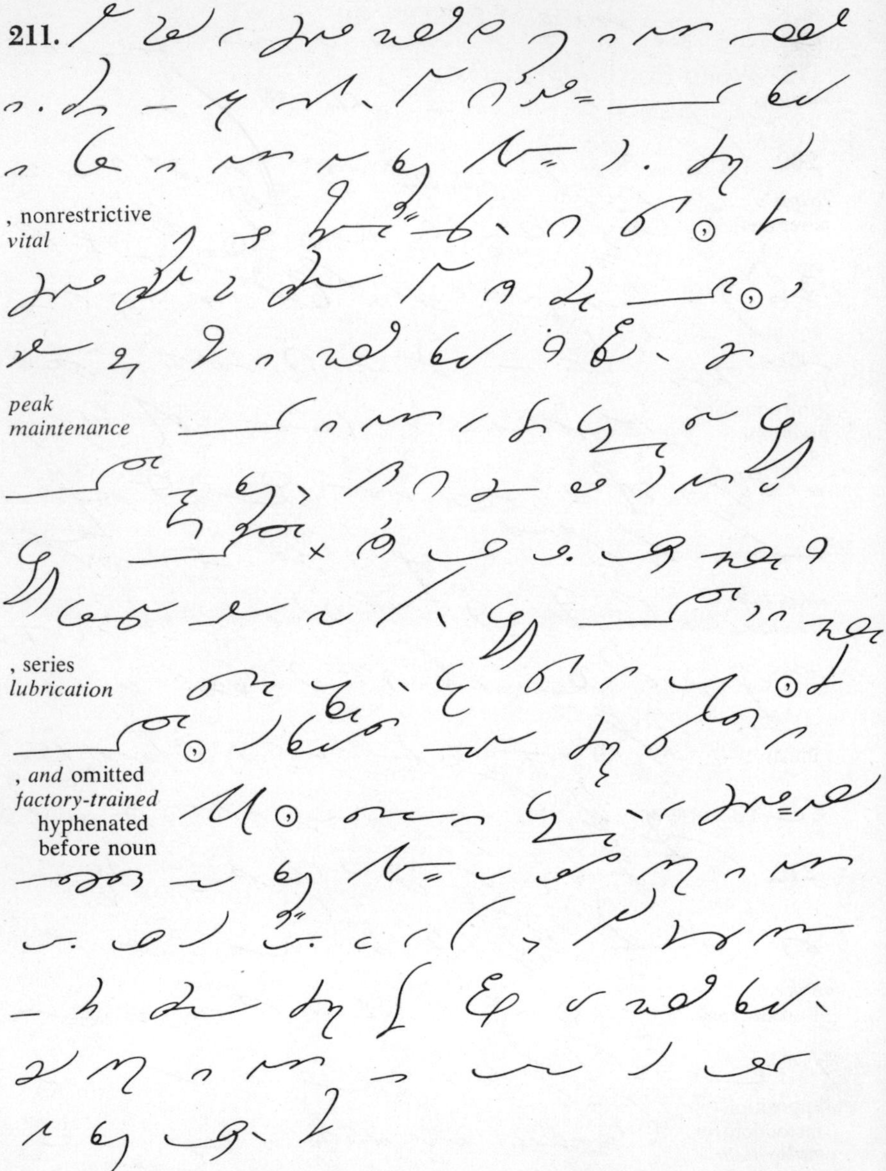

[shorthand outlines]

, nonrestrictive
vital

[shorthand outlines]

peak
maintenance

[shorthand outlines]

, series
lubrication

[shorthand outlines]

, *and* omitted
factory-trained
hyphenated
before noun

[shorthand outlines]

LESSON 30

212. WORD-BUILDING PRACTICE—VOWEL COMBINATIONS

IA, EA

YE, YA

DOUBLE CIRCLE

OE, EO

Key

Area, create, bacteria, cafeteria, aviation, appreciate, civilian.
Yell, yellow, yield, yearn, Yale, yarn.
Riot, diet, quiet, science, appliance, diamond, violin.
Poem, poet, poetry, folio, portfolio, radio.

213. ACCURACY PRACTICE—PROPORTION

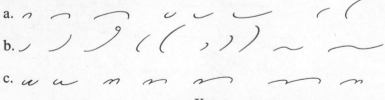

a.

b.

c.

Key

a. You, your; can; go, good; of; our, are, hour; will, well; the; time.
b. There, their; and, end; empty; put; be, by; is, his; for; have; correct; glad.
c. Of all, of our, world, you can, you go, can go, can you.

READING AND WRITING PRACTICE

214. The Automobile

dominion
humanity
radius

subtle
ambition
peace

, conjunction
isolated

silent
man's

, series
adventure
recreation

stifling
murmuring

reunion
supremacy

[shorthand]

—*John O. Munn*

215. The Boy Who Put The World On Wheels

[shorthand]

, conjunction
machinery

[shorthand]

, introducing
   short quote
? inside quote

[shorthand]

chores
lantern

[shorthand]

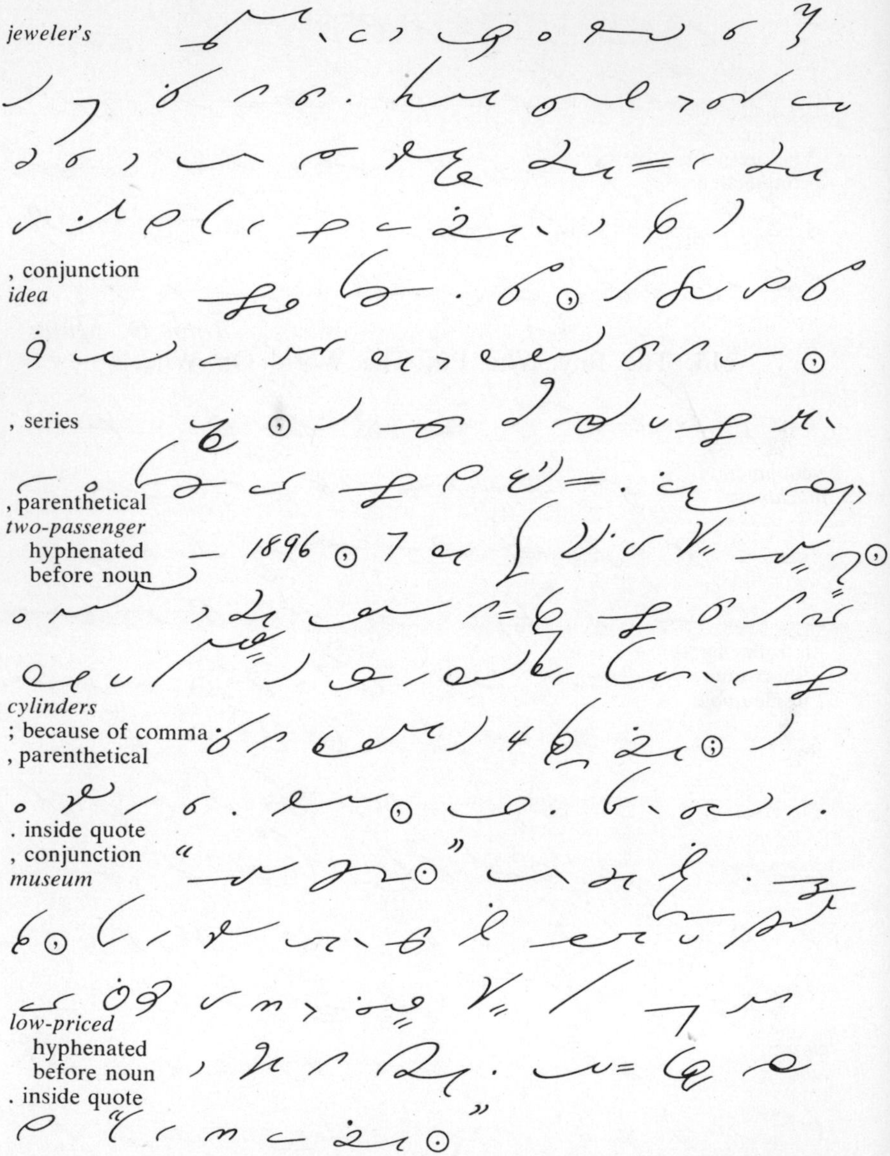

jeweler's

, conjunction
idea

, series

, parenthetical
two-passenger
hyphenated
before noun

cylinders
; because of comma
, parenthetical

. inside quote
, conjunction
museum

low-priced
hyphenated
before noun
. inside quote

216. Let's Tell The Worker Why

pick-and-shovel
hyphenated
before noun
, conjunction

repeated
, parenthetical

burst
, conjunction

, series
community
government

, series
freely

, *and* omitted

, introductory
grievance
procedure

LESSON 31

217. WORD FAMILIES

-UATE

-UATION

-IER

-SIVE

-KEN

Key

Evaluate, extenuate, insinuate, perpetuate, graduate.

Evaluation, extenuation, insinuation, perpetuation, graduation.

Busier, earlier, funnier, nastier, happier, heavier, prettier, fancier.

Extensive, expensive, impressive, defensive, comprehensive, offensive, impulsive.

Darken, thicken, taken, quicken, spoken, awaken, weaken.

READING AND WRITING PRACTICE

218. *[shorthand outlines]*

Transcribe:
8:55 a.m.
; no conjunction

[shorthand outlines]

: enumeration
, series
, *when* clause
St. Louis

[shorthand outlines]

newly revised
no hyphen
after *ly*

[shorthand outlines]

219.

Men's
Tailors
personnel

[shorthand outlines]

worth while
no noun,
no hyphen

[shorthand outlines]

description
, *if* clause

220.
Aeronautics
, introductory
, *if* clause

effective
intervene

, *if* clause
separate
attorneys

. *courteous*
request

221.
, nonrestrictive
gasoline
planes

CHAPTER VII

facilities
, *as* clause
; illustrative ,
, series

, *and* omitted
awkward
refuel

, *when* clause
, parenthetical
installation

postpone
immediately

222.

, *and* omitted
large-sized
  hyphenated
  before noun
, nonrestrictive

arrival
, conjunction

184

bearing
possibility
, conjunction

Northern
, apposition
; because of comma

, *if* clause

223.
coupons
Columbus
Cleveland
reimbursement

, *as* clause

5:30

4:30

CHAPTER VII

, parenthetical
knowledge
awaken

; because of
  comma
, *if* clause.

, conjunction
enjoyable

224.
  , year date
  , introducing
      short quote

1953

. inside quote
appreciative

urging

LESSON 32

225. Brief-Form Derivatives

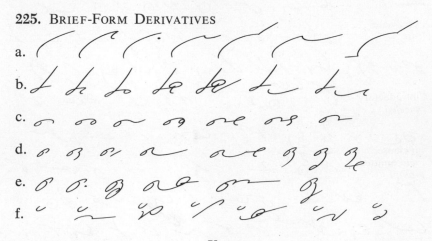

Key

a. Time, times, timing, timer, timed, timeless, untimed.

b. General, generals, generally, generalize, generalized, generality, generalities.

c. Weak, weakly, weaker, weakest, weakness, weaknesses, weaken.

d. Use, uses, used, useless, uselessness, useful, usefully, usefulness.

e. Out, outing, outside, outline, outcome, outfit.

f. Over, overcome, overstay, overdue, override, overcoat, oversee.

226. Geographical Expressions

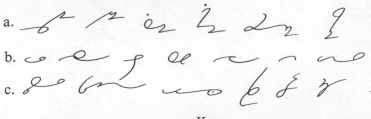

Key

a. Madison, Dawson, Harrison, Hutchinson, Ferguson, Atchison.

b. Oregon, California, Nevada, Arizona, Colorado, Kansas, Oklahoma.

c. Italy, Portugal, Romania, Japan, Spain, Sweden.

READING AND WRITING PRACTICE

227. *[shorthand outlines]*

, year date
lease

; introductory
canceled

, *if* clause
, *and* omitted
prompt

228. *[shorthand outlines]*

, parenthetical
daily

, nonrestrictive
first-class
  hyphenated
  before noun

one-way
round-trip
  hyphenated
  before noun
; no conjunction

, introductory *(shorthand outline)*

6-2596

229. *(shorthand outline)*

; illustrative ,
, series
luxury

(shorthand outlines)

, conjunction

(shorthand outlines)

employees
union
, *if* clause

(shorthand outlines)

: enumeration
, series
summary

(shorthand outlines)

. courteous
request

(shorthand outlines)

230.

cancellation
reservation

180

(shorthand outlines)

CHAPTER VII

receiving
, introductory

advise
, apposition

, introducing
  short quote
. inside quote
exceptions

, parenthetical

, parenthetical
compensate

, conjunction
similar

231.

badly damaged
  no hyphen
  after *ly*
Smith's

, as clause
assignment
Directors

, parenthetical

, introductory
length

232.

, *when* clause
schedules

233.

encountered
unfortunate

CHAPTER VII

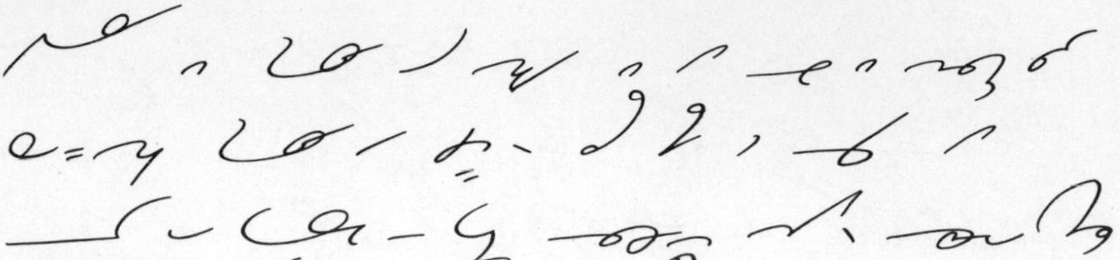

, parenthetical
occasionally
incurred

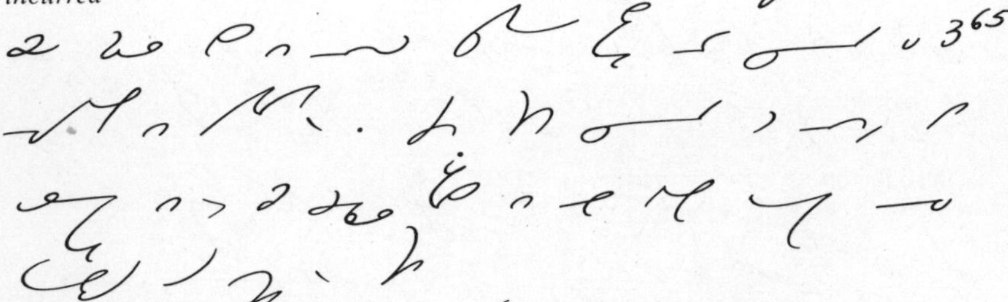

234.

, *when* clause
carried

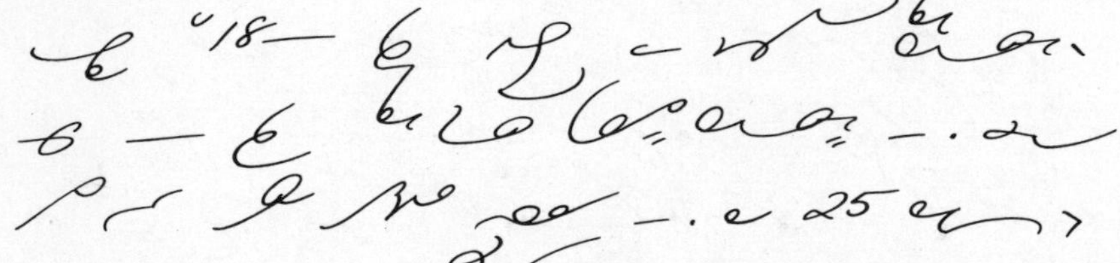

, introductory

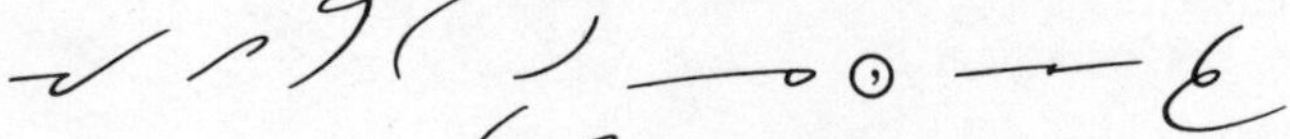

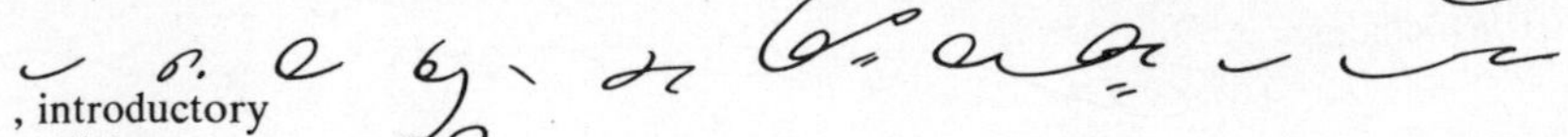

, introductory
well known
no noun,
no hyphen

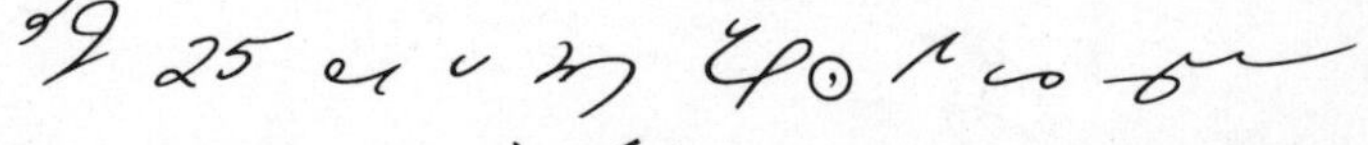

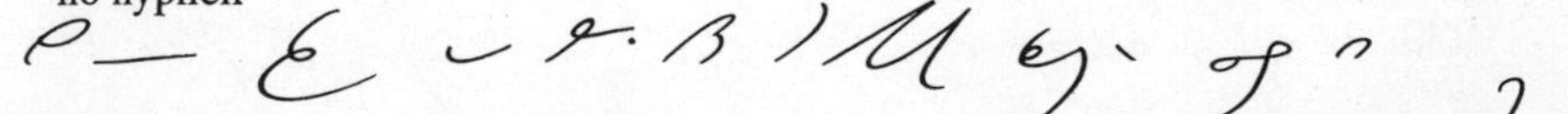

, introductory

LESSON 33

235. USEFUL BUSINESS-LETTER PHRASES

AT

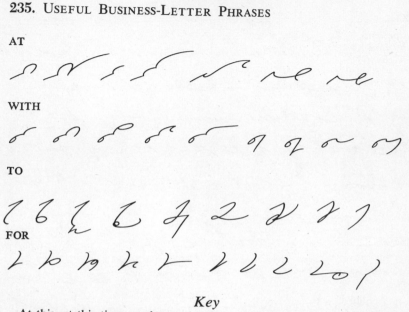

WITH

TO

FOR

Key

At this, at this time, at the, at the time, at all times, at last, at least.

With the, with this, with that, with those, with them, with which, with which the, with our, with reference.

To be, to be able, to be sure, to build, to change, to feel, to find, to fit, to have.

For the, for that, for these, for those, for them, for it, for their, for our, for my, for which.

236. FREQUENT NAMES

a.

b.

Key

a. Graham, Griffiths, Hamilton, Hanson, Harris.
b. Dorothy, Edith, Edna, Eleanor, Elizabeth, Esther.

CHAPTER VII

READING AND WRITING PRACTICE

237.

experience
instruments
overhaul

[shorthand outlines]

, when clause

[shorthand outlines]

, and omitted
co-operation

[shorthand outlines]

, conjunction

[shorthand outlines]

238.

refueling
New Orleans

[shorthand outlines]

, introductory
, parenthetical

[shorthand outlines]

194

[Shorthand outlines]

, introducing
   short quote
. inside quote

[Shorthand outlines]

, conjunction

[Shorthand outlines]

; because of comma
, introductory
decision

[Shorthand outlines]

, conjunction
equitable

[Shorthand outlines]

239.
forwarded
, apposition
; illustrative ,

[Shorthand outlines]

, *as* clause
mishandled

[Shorthand outlines]

, introductory
, parenthetical

[Shorthand outlines]

CHAPTER VII

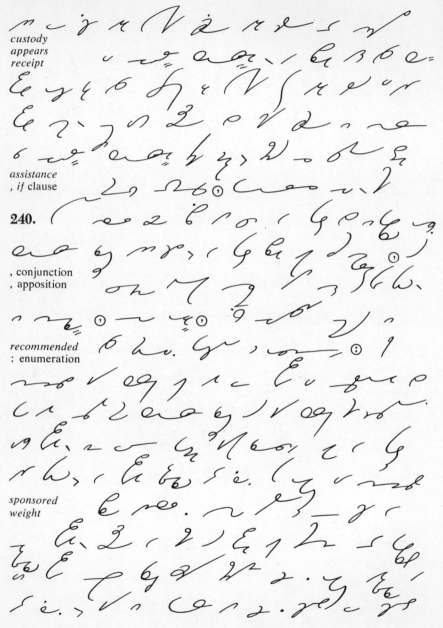

custody
appears
receipt

assistance
, if clause

240.

, conjunction
, apposition

recommended
: enumeration

sponsored
weight

, introductory
arranging

[shorthand outlines]

witnesses
, apposition
; because of comma

241.

correcting
mechanical
Flight

, introductory
schedule
accept

fine-spirited
hyphenated
before noun

, series
attendants

; no conjunction
efficiently run
no hyphen
after *ly*

197

CHAPTER VII

242.

Hart's
received
via

, introductory
personnel

, nonrestrictive
, conjunction

, conjunction

. courteous
request

198

LESSON 34

243. Word Beginnings

SUB-

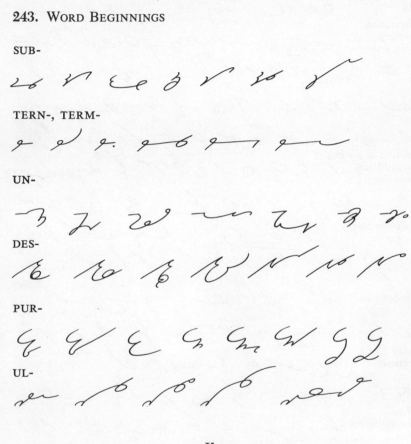

TERN-, TERM-

UN-

DES-

PUR-

UL-

Key

Submit, substantial, sublease, subway, subdue, substitute, subeditor.
Turn, turned, turning, terminate, termination, terminal.
Unconscious, unchecked, unfriendly, unlock, unpolished, unwise, unwittingly.
Despair, desperate, despise, despondent, destined, destitute, destiny.
Purport, purported, purple, pursue, pursuance, pursued, purvey, purveyor.
Ulterior, ultimate, ultimately, ultimatum, ultramodern.

READING AND WRITING PRACTICE

244.
, apposition
Transcribe:
No. 4680

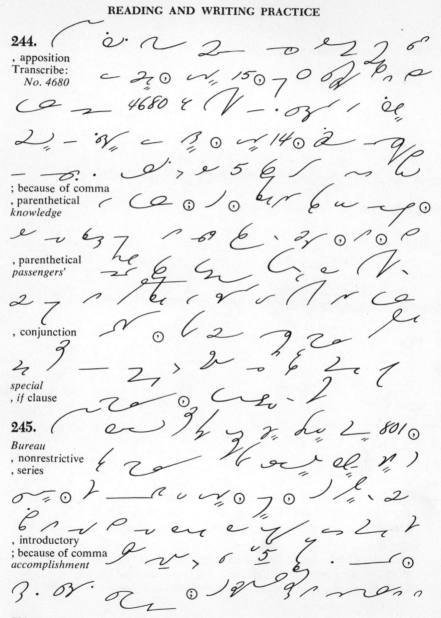

; because of comma
, parenthetical
knowledge

, parenthetical
passengers'

, conjunction

special
, *if* clause

245.
Bureau
, nonrestrictive
, series

, introductory
; because of comma
accomplishment

[Shorthand outlines]

246.

, *as* clause
Aeronautics

: introducing
  long quote
. inside quote

, introductory

, introductory
further

days'
, introductory

, parenthetical

247.

, introducing
  short quote
. inside quote

, parenthetical
, apposition
co-operation

amazing
, parenthetical

, *and* omitted
pieces

248.

Minnesota
aviation

small-capacity
hyphenated
before noun
; no conjunction

replenish
Rochester's

, *if* clause
: enumeration

fully loaded
no hyphen
after *ly*

249.

Director
assistance

CHAPTER VII

, introductory
appeared
decentralize

; illustrative ,
, series
authorization

inasmuch as
up to date
no noun,
no hyphen

, when clause
activities

LESSON 35

250. WORD-BUILDING PRACTICE—OMISSION OF *t* AND *d*

T IN SEVEN MONOSYLLABLES

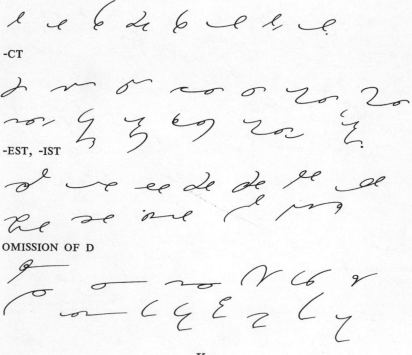

-CT

-EST, -IST

OMISSION OF D

Key

Test, rest, best, first, past, last, tested, lasting.

Fact, contract, attract, collect, act, reflect, conflict, connected, projects, respective, selective, reflector, self-respecting.

Kindest, longest, nearest, fairest, finest, dearest, latest, capitalist, chemist, humorist, dentist, druggist.

Diamond, amend, command, dividend, pretend, extend, demand, recommend, pound, propound, expound, compound, bound, rebound.

READING AND WRITING PRACTICE

251. A Trip To Europe By Plane

[Shorthand content]

, parenthetical
millions

far-off
hyphenated
before noun
, series

previously
appeal

war ravaged
no noun,
no hyphen

, series
customs
costumes

all-too-short
hyphenated
before noun

pursuits
byways

transoceanic

, and omitted
attractive
delicious

congenial
atmosphere
, introductory

, introductory
; because of comma

, introductory
taxi

CHAPTER VII

, parenthetical
foreign

, introductory
Seine

wealthy

, parenthetical
language

barrier
beware
, introductory

hairbreadth
, conjunction

careens
, *as* clause
, *if* clause
vehicle

[Shorthand notation fills the page]

, parenthetical
historic

Mona Lisa
mystic
, parenthetical

boulevards
, introductory

cafés
Parisians
, introductory
, series

, *if* clause

, *and* omitted
beverage
accompanied

, *if* clause
tempted
creation

souvenirs
amazed

, *if* clause
limitation

first class
no noun,
no hyphen

, *parenthetical*

—*Flora Stenzil*

CHAPTER **VIII**

LESSON 36

252. WORD FAMILIES

-IATE

[shorthand outlines]

-IANCE

[shorthand outlines]

-IAL

[shorthand outlines]

-ION

[shorthand outlines]

-CY, -SY

[shorthand outlines]

Key
Appreciate, substantiate, negotiate, initiate, associate, officiate.
Alliance, appliance, reliance, compliance, self-reliance.
Serial, material, aerial, burial, industrial.
Million, billion, dominion, companion, union, onion.
Secrecy, diplomacy, courtesy, fallacy, lunacy, accuracy.

CHAPTER VIII

READING AND WRITING PRACTICE

253.

candidates
bachelor's

, introductory
Transcribe:
$2,900

29)

, parenthetical
beginning

33)

150/   58)

master's
, introductory

62)

254.

, conjunction
applicant

212

, introductory
stenographer

human
; illustrative ,
, series

, series
faculty
officials

practical
, as clause

qualifications
, introductory

255.

gratifying

, apposition
, *if* clause
convenient

; no conjunction
schedule

256.

, apposition
encouraging
facilities

well-planned
hyphenated
before noun
, *and* omitted

fully equipped
no hyphen
after *ly*

257.

, introducing
  short quote
its

214

[Shorthand outlines]

. inside quote
morning's

, *when* clause
, introductory
instructional
materials

258.

, introductory
; because of comma
, nonrestrictive

259.

worth while
no noun,
no hyphen
, parenthetical

260.

judgment
ideal
experience

well-organized
hyphenated
before noun

phase
, *if* clause

LESSON 37

261. BRIEF-FORM DERIVATIVES

Key

a. Long, longing, longed, longer, longingly, longs.
b. Deliver, delivers, delivering, delivery, deliverable, undeliverable.
c. Desire, desired, desiring, desires, desirable, undesirable, desirability.
d. Please, pleasing, pleasingly, pleased, pleases, displease.
e. Date, dating, dates, dated, dateline, undated.
f. End, ending, ends, ended, endless, endlessly, unending.

262. GEOGRAPHICAL EXPRESSIONS

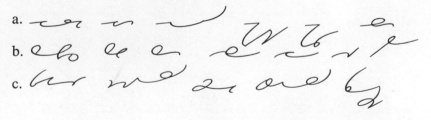

Key

a. New Orleans, New York, New London, New Bedford, New Britain, Newark.

b. Alaska, Arizona, Arkansas, California, Colorado, Connecticut, Delaware.

c. Portsmouth, Scotland, Wales, Ireland, Belfast.

CHAPTER VIII

READING AND WRITING PRACTICE

263.

, introductory
secretarial

, apposition
part-time
hyphenated
before noun

, series
practice

, introductory
; because of comma
clients

, year date
until

experience
exceedingly
, and omitted
, introductory

218

264.

recommendation
senior
, *as* clause

some time
interview

265.

, introducing
short quote
, *if* clause

worth while
no noun,
no hyphen
. inside quote

, *as* clause
beneficial
career

, nonrestrictive
junior
majored

, conjunction
, introductory
proficient
calculating

part-time
hyphenated
before noun

. courteous
request
, introductory

266.

, apposition

weeks'
secretaries

220

; no conjunction
, introductory
period

, parenthetical
worth while
 no noun,
 no hyphen

, *when* clause

4-5322

267.

recommended
assist
, conjunction

possesses
; illustrative ,
, series

, introductory

268.

; because of comma
, if clause

, introductory

, if clause
: enumeration
proceed

photograph
acquainted

LESSON 38

269. USEFUL BUSINESS-LETTER PHRASES

TO

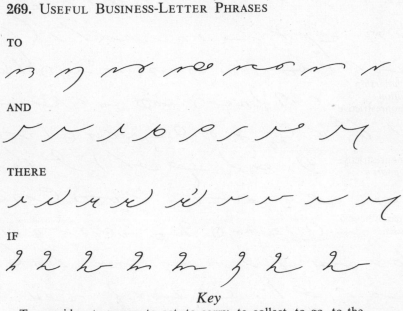

AND

THERE

IF

Key

To consider, to cover, to get, to carry, to collect, to go, to the.

And are, and will, and is, and say, and that, and the, and let, and will be.

There is, there is not, there was, there was not, there wasn't, there are, there are not, there will, there will be.

If you, if you are, if you are not, if you can, if you cannot, if you have, if you will, if you will not.

270. FREQUENT NAMES

a.

b.

Key

a. Henderson, Hoffman, Hughes, Hunter, Jackson, Johnson, Johnston.

b. Felix, Francis, Frederick, George, Gilbert, Godfrey.

READING AND WRITING PRACTICE

271.

[shorthand outlines]

scholarship
tuition
, nonrestrictive

[shorthand outlines]

, nonrestrictive
support

[shorthand outlines]

, parenthetical
basis

[shorthand outlines]

, *if* clause
whether

[shorthand outlines]

uncle's
relaxation
, series

[shorthand outlines]

272.

[shorthand outlines]

, *and* omitted
nationally known
no hyphen
after *ly*

thorough
, series

, *if* clause
splendid

; illustrative ,
, series
salary

273.

, introductory
, apposition
attractive

, introductory
believe
possess

[shorthand notes]

, *when* clause
, introducing
short quote
. inside quote

[shorthand notes]

274.

participation
trainee

[shorthand notes]

, *as* clause

[shorthand notes]

, introductory
graduation

[shorthand notes]

: enumeration

[shorthand notes]

transcriptions
, introductory

background
bookkeeping
key-punch

, apposition
, if clause
choice

275.

well-established
  hyphenated
  before noun

permanent
, introductory
; because of comma

30

America's
commission

276.

forward
. courteous
  request

LESSON 39

277. WORD ENDINGS

-GRAM

-HOOD

-IFICATION

-INGLY

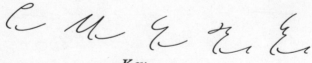

-INGS

-LITY

Key

Program, diagram, monogram, radiogram, telegram.

Neighborhood, parenthood, childhood, adulthood, priesthood, manhood.

Notification, modification, fortification, gratification, ratification, specification, specifications.

Willingly, seemingly, surprisingly, entertainingly, grudgingly, jokingly.

Feelings, engravings, shavings, greetings, castings, mornings.

Facility, ability, dependability, probability, sensibilities, possibilities.

READING AND WRITING PRACTICE

278.

worth-while
  hyphenated
  before noun
city's
, nonrestrictive

, apposition
employees

, when clause
pledges

279.

, nonrestrictive
acknowledged

, as clause
Transcribe:
  $300

. courteous
  request
, if clause
, parenthetical

280.

well-trained
hyphenated
before noun
, conjunction

[shorthand outlines]

; no conjunction
, introductory
nevertheless

[shorthand outlines]

, conjunction
, introductory

[shorthand outlines]

, year date
, nonrestrictive
inside quote

[shorthand outlines] ○ 1953 ○ *[shorthand outlines]*

281.

[shorthand outlines]

, *and* omitted
, series

, introducing
short quote
. inside quote

Transcribe:
50 cents
offered

282.
, nonrestrictive
formerly
associated

accept
, introductory

, conjunction
lose

Barry's
: enumeration

; because of comma
, *if* clause
asset

283.

nonpayment
. inside quote

, *as* clause
past due
  no noun,
  no hyphen

, introductory
repeated

[shorthand outlines]

, introductory
attorney

procedure
embarrassment
unfavorable

284.

previous
, nonrestrictive

, parenthetical

past-due
hyphenated
before noun

, parenthetical

LESSON 40

285. WORD-BUILDING PRACTICE—OMISSION OF VOWELS

-TATION, ETC.

[shorthand outlines]

-EST, -IST FOLLOWING A VOWEL

[shorthand outlines]

OMISSION OF OW

[shorthand outlines]

Key

Station, sanitation, interpretation, condition, expedition, addition, foundation, inclination, termination, condemnation, summation, formation, information.

Highest, happiest, loveliest, prettiest, fanciest, daintiest, wealthiest, steadiest, friendliest, easiest, essayist, newest, lowest.

Announce, announcement, council, councilor, sound, found.

286. ACCURACY PRACTICE—O HOOK

a. *[shorthand outlines]*

b. *[shorthand outlines]*

Key

a. Of, was, hope, object, row, low, toe, no, most.
b. What, order, or, coal, body, saw, of course, organize.

CHAPTER VIII

READING AND WRITING PRACTICE

287. Selling Yourself

commodity
possess
endurance

, parenthetical
resistance
overwhelming

; no conjunction
answered

, if clause
; illustrative ,

: enumeration
, series

combination
, series

[Shorthand notes]

, *when* clause
brevity
completeness

, *if* clause

, series
employer's

, parenthetical
survey

, parenthetical

, parenthetical

clinic
advises
success

: enumeration
, series

, *when* clause
screen

: enumeration
, series

: enumeration
summary

, parenthetical
, if clause

offer
total
, introductory

, introductory
sight

its
, conjunction

contact
, if clause

, parenthetical
single
qualifies

opposite
, conjunction

busiest
, introductory

initiative
, introductory

PART II

CHAPTERS 9-16

CHAPTER IX

LESSON 41

288. WORD FAMILIES

-NMENT

-SCRIPTION

-PLE

-NESS

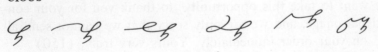

-CIOUS

Key

Assignment, confinement, refinement, adjournment, consignment, imprisonment.

Inscription, prescription, description, conscription, transcription, subscription.

Simple, sample, example, triple, disciple.

Laziness, happiness, uneasiness, costliness, illness, cheerfulness.

Precious, gracious, malicious, fallacious, delicious, atrocious.

CHAPTER IX

289. PREVIEW AND WRITING PRACTICE

PREVIEW FOR LETTER **290.**

[shorthand outlines]

Key

Thank you for your, substantial, conclude, volume, we hope that.
Suites, few days, breakfast, leather, available, it has been, continues.
Popularity, quickly, your order, we want, patronage, items, immediately.

290. Dear Mr. Roberts: Thank you for your spring order. As it is the most substantial order you have ever sent us,[1] we conclude that your volume of sales must be very good. We hope that you will have a constantly increasing volume[2] of sales throughout the year.

The bedroom suites, the living-room suites, and the tables can be shipped within the next few[3] days. The breakfast sets and the leather chairs, however, will not be available for two weeks.

Our rug supply, which[4] is larger than it has been at any time in recent years, continues to lead the field in popularity.[5] If you need extra supplies of rugs in any size, we can quickly fill your order.

We want to take this opportunity[6] to thank you for your continued patronage, and we are only sorry that we cannot send all items[7] on your order immediately. Yours very truly, (150)

READING AND WRITING PRACTICE

291. *[shorthand outlines]*

suites
: enumeration

, parenthetical
Transcribe:
   No. 486

292.

; illustrative ,
breakfast

; no conjunction
grateful

293.

, parenthetical
accordance

remainder
merchandise

294. *[shorthand outline]*

arrival
, when clause

[shorthand outline]

, introducing
short quote
, year date   1927
. inside quote

[shorthand outline]

, introducing
short quote
. inside quote
, parenthetical

company's
high-quality
hyphenated
before noun

[shorthand outline]   485

[shorthand outline]   891   987.

295. *[shorthand outline]*   1910

, as clause
men's
, introductory

[shorthand outline]

ladies'
wear

[shorthand outline]

, series
precision

, conjunction
equally

, *and* omitted
excellent
, series

ready-to-wear
  hyphenated
  before noun
, introductory

296.

, series

exhibit
beginning

, parenthetical
drawers

CHAPTER IX

[Shorthand notes]

, introductory
surprisingly

, *if* clause
; because of comma
definitely

297.

, *as* clause
; no conjunction
, introductory

happier
, introductory

; because of comma
, introductory

248

LESSON 42

298. BRIEF-FORM DERIVATIVES

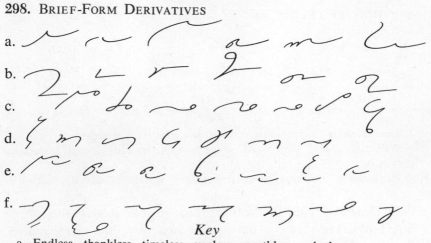

Key

a. Endless, thankless, timeless, useless, worthless, valueless.

b. Government, shipment, statement, advertisement, acknowledgment, accompaniment.

c. Directly, generally, gladly, greatly, correctly, orderly, probably.

d. Objection, succession, organization, presentation, satisfaction, conclusion, correction.

e. Director, outer, user, believer, worker, speaker, thinker.

f. Uncovered, unbusinesslike, unworkable, unimportant, unsuccessful, unlike, unsatisfactory.

299. GEOGRAPHICAL EXPRESSIONS

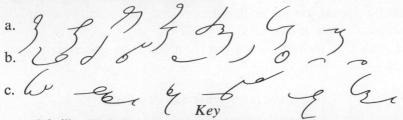

Key

a. Ashville, Nashville, Danville, Evansville, Jacksonville, Brownsville, Knoxville.

b. Florida, Georgia, Idaho, Illinois, Indiana, Iowa, Kansas, Kentucky.

c. Bordeaux, Marseilles, Cherbourg, Madrid, Lisbon, Brussels.

249

CHAPTER IX

300. PREVIEW AND WRITING PRACTICE

PREVIEW FOR LETTER 301.

Key

This morning, merchandise, previously, inactivity, wonder.

We have done, patronized, infrequently, instead, frankly, trouble, prompted.

Discontinue, won't, personally, recently, envelope, directly, forward.

301. Dear Mrs. Hill: In checking through your account this morning, I observed that you have purchased very little merchandise[1] from us for the past 90 days. Previously, your account showed a steady sales record. The present inactivity[2] of your account causes me to wonder what we have done or what has happened that you have patronized[3] our store so infrequently in the last three months.

Instead of continuing to wonder about your lack of purchases,[4] I have decided to ask you frankly just what the trouble is or what we have done that may have prompted[5] you to discontinue buying from our store. Won't you please write me personally on the back of this letter and[6] tell me why you have not been buying from us recently. Please use the enclosed envelope, as I want your reply[7] to come directly to my desk.

I shall look forward to hearing from you soon. Sincerely yours, (156)

READING AND WRITING PRACTICE

302.

enclosed
, parenthetical

250

as clause
past due
  no noun,
  no hyphen

, *when* clause
receipt

; because of comma
, parenthetical
received

, *if* clause
, introductory

303.

, introductory
wisely

, parenthetical
; illustrative ,

high-quality
  hyphenated
  before noun

everyone
, series
: enumeration

, series
surgery

; no conjunction
, *when* clause

recipe
budget

favorite
, *when* clause

304.

; because of comma
, introductory
acquaintances

, year date
, parenthetical

1940

, introductory
likewise
predecessors

, series
entertainment

, *as* clause
postpone

305.

, nonrestrictive
unique
delicious

, parenthetical
, *and* omitted
ready-to-use
  hyphenated
  before noun

; because of comma
, introducing
  short quote

[Shorthand content]

. inside quote
recently revised
no hyphen
after *ly*

. inside quote

306.

Ryan's
, introductory

, series
loveliest

, conjunction
rug-making
hyphenated
before noun

choice
colors

LESSON 43

307. USEFUL BUSINESS-LETTER PHRASES

DO

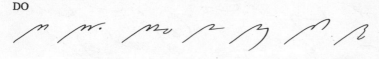

HAS

IS

PLEASE

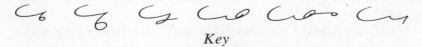

Key

Do you, do you think, do you know, do not, do not have, do this, do so.
Has the, has not, has not yet, has not yet been, has come, has done, has had.
Is the, is that, is that the, is this, is not, isn't, is made, is to be.
Please see, please pay, please send, please write, please write me, please rush.

308. FREQUENT NAMES

a.

b.

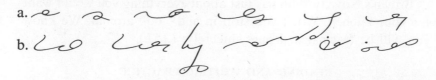

Key

a. Kerr, King, Klein, Larsen, Levy, Lynch.
b. Flora, Florence, Georgiana, Gertrude, Harriet, Henrietta.

CHAPTER IX

309. Preview and Writing Practice

PREVIEW FOR LETTER 310.

Key

Practical, knickknacks, soaring, colorful.
Unique, wooden, shelves, utensils, cabinet, utility, surrounded.
Old-world, atmosphere, Novelty, everything, won't, fascinated.

310. Dear Mrs. Sweet: Would you like to know how you can make your kitchen the type of room in which it is a pleasure to[1] work? Getting some pretty, practical knickknacks will give you a lift, will send your spirits soaring, and will give you a[2] new lease on life.

If you are looking for colorful pottery to brighten your wall, you will find some unique pieces[3] at Brown's. Perhaps you might like one of those new wooden hanging shelves on which you can place gay plates and hook on kitchen[4] utensils.

Perhaps you would like a spice cabinet. You cannot equal the charm and utility of a[5] spice cabinet on your kitchen wall. This cabinet, surrounded by copper pans, will lend an old-world atmosphere[6] to your kitchen.

Brown's Novelty Shop has just about everything you would want for your kitchen. Won't you stop in and[7] look around. We know you will be fascinated. Yours sincerely, (151)

READING AND WRITING PRACTICE

311.

[Shorthand notes]

, year date
reality

, conjunction
gray

, series
rinses

: introducing
long quote
, introductory

thoroughness
inside quote

demonstration
; no conjunction

312.

imagination
; no conjunction
, introductory

extravagant
offering

ideas
, introductory
, series

313.

, introductory
prominent
role

clothes
, *as* clause

, nonrestrictive
women's

; because of comma
developing

: enumeration
, series
functions

, apposition
occasion

314.

, apposition
welcome

, introductory
, *and* omitted
, series
high-quality
  hyphenated
  before noun

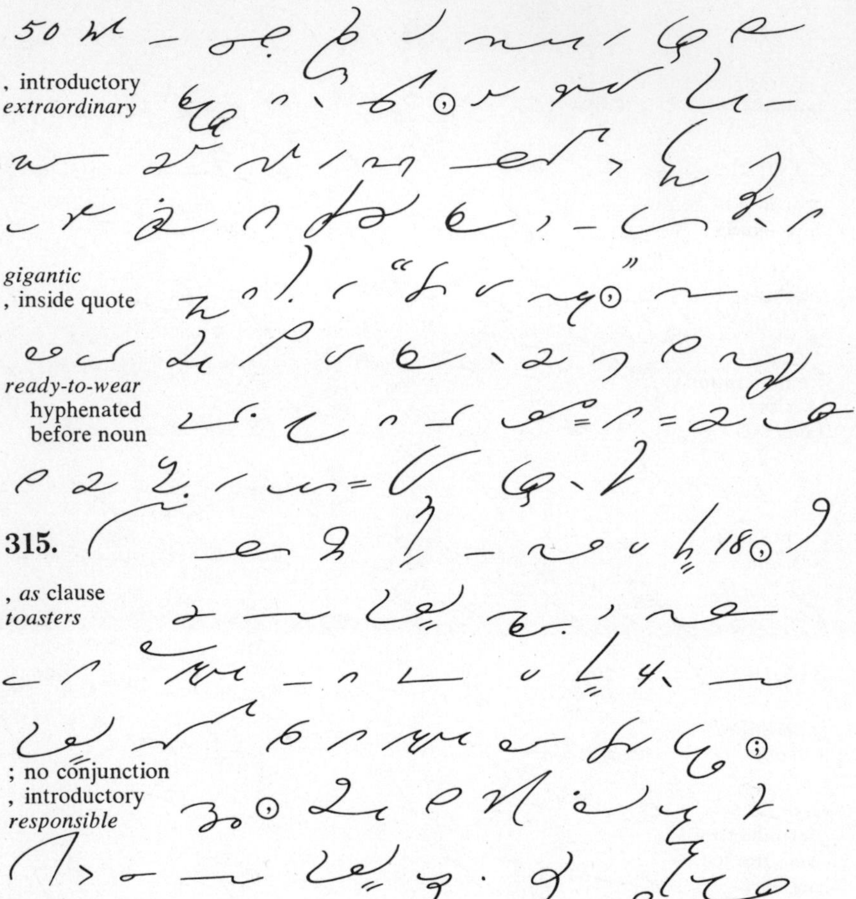
, introductory
extraordinary
gigantic
, inside quote
ready-to-wear
hyphenated
before noun
315.
, *as* clause
toasters
; no conjunction
, introductory
responsible
, *when* clause
draft
, conjunction
judgment
recommend

LESSON 44

316. Word Beginnings

ELECTRIC-

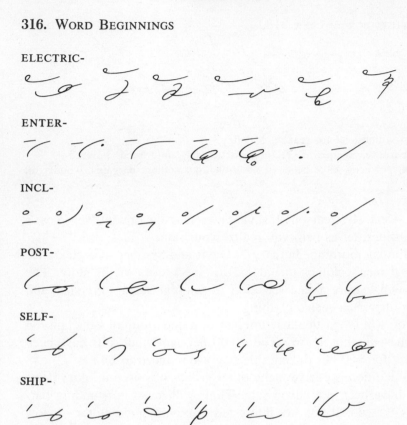

ENTER-

INCL-

POST-

SELF-

SHIP-

Key

Electric light, electric fan, electric wire, electric motor, electric razor, electric switch.

Entertain, entertaining, entertainment, enterprise, enterprisingly, entering, entered.

Incline, inclined, inclines, inclination, include, includes, including, included.

Postman, postmaster, postal, post card, postpone, postponement.

Self-made, self-confidence, self-analysis, selfish, selfishness, self-reliance.

Shipmate, shipwreck, shipyard, shipshape, shipowner, shipbuilder.

CHAPTER IX

317. PREVIEW AND WRITING PRACTICE

PREVIEW FOR LETTER 318.

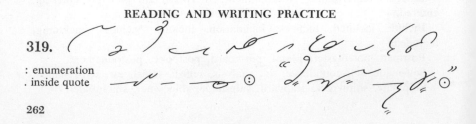

Key

Resolutions, let us, realize, Monday.

Clearance, unequaled, feature, particularly, interested, tailored.

100 per cent, have been, in addition, outstanding, bargains, wonderful, next.

318. Dear Mr. Pearson: If saving money is one of your New Year's resolutions, let us help you realize your[1] aim.

Monday morning, January 7, Davis and Son begins a clearance sale of men's clothes unequaled in[2] the history of the store. The sale will feature a fine selection of popular suits, top coats, and other items[3] in men's clothing.

You will be particularly interested in one group of suits tailored for the tall, slim figure.[4] These 100 per cent wool suits have been selling for $60 but during this sale are reduced to $43.[5]

In addition, we have many other groups of suits and other items that have been placed on sale. That[6] will mean outstanding bargains for you. If you are interested in buying good clothes at low prices, you will not miss[7] this wonderful sale.

Plan now to come in next Monday morning. Yours very cordially, (155)

READING AND WRITING PRACTICE

319.

: enumeration
. inside quote

262

, year date
; because of comma
gravely

1952

bearing
, series

fault
, *if* clause

320.

; because of comma
, parenthetical
  inside quote

, series
fair
unexcelled

lost
, conjunction

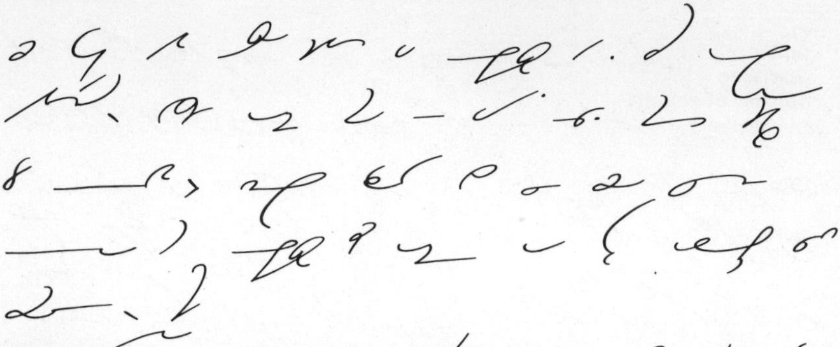

321.

unnecessary
past
gratifying

reasonable
, series

, *when* clause
dissatisfaction
repetition

322.

, *if* clause
, *and* omitted
cheerful

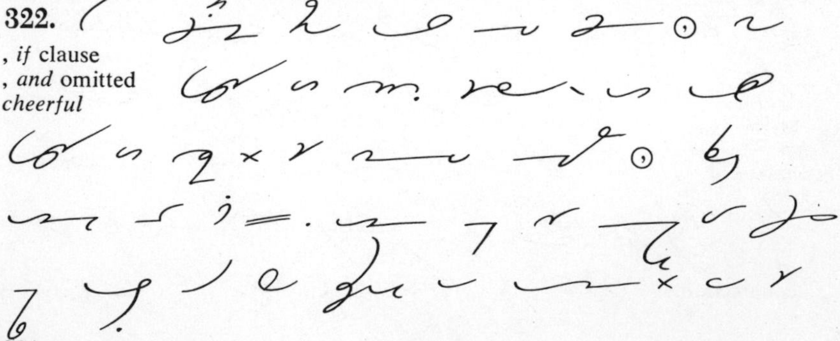

, *and* omitted
, *if* clause

overlooked
, series

, introductory
science

, series
family
coupon

; no conjunction
touch

323.
, apposition
, introducing
  short quote

. inside quote
catalogue

, parenthetical
, nonrestrictive
, *as* clause
, series

CHAPTER IX

(shorthand outlines)

324.

: enumeration
interpret
budgeting

, apposition
discussed

, parenthetical

adapt
; illustrative ,
, series

, *if clause*
review

worth while
  no noun,
  no hyphen

LESSON 45

325. WORD-BUILDING PRACTICE — DIPHTHONGS

I

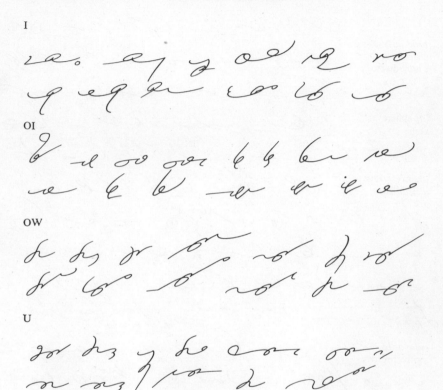

OI

OW

U

Key

Smilingly, mileage, resign, island, trifle, strike, liable, reliable, tireless, slightly, frighten, lighten.

Avoid, noise, annoy, annoyance, choice, choices, boiler, toiled, royal, poison, joined, moisture, oyster, hoist, oily.

Power, powerful, south, doubtless, crowd, vouch, scouted, powdered, proudly, undoubtedly, clouds, shower, mouths.

Execute, furious, refuge, purely, arguments, accumulated, cure, curious, document, fewer, graduate.

CHAPTER IX

READING AND WRITING PRACTICE

326. Retail Selling

product's
crucial
, introductory

, if clause
vain

, nonrestrictive
distribution

enjoyable
, introductory

high-pressure
hyphenated
before noun
, nonrestrictive

[Shorthand content]

, conjunction
firm's

customer's
intangible
visible

, introductory
possess

, series
merchandise

, parenthetical

: enumeration
, series
indifference

CHAPTER IX

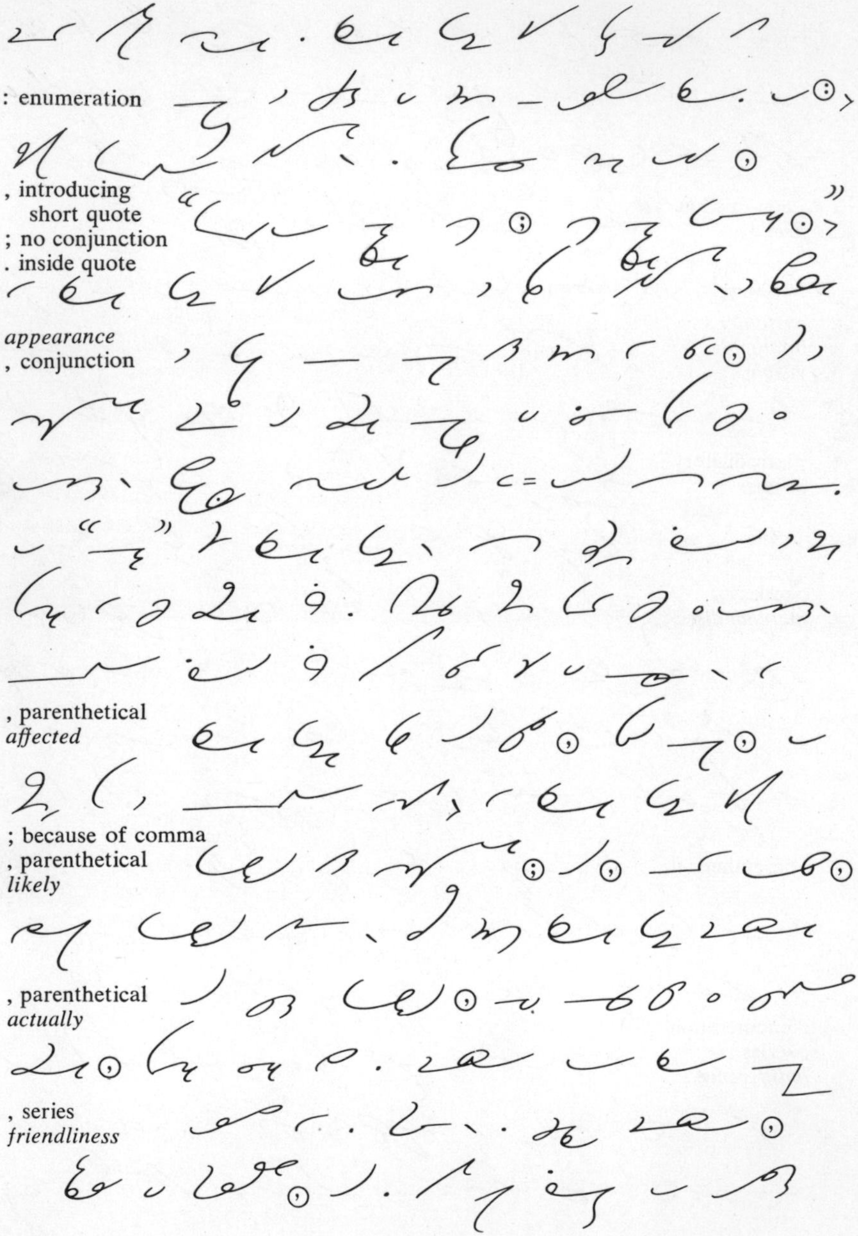
: enumeration
, introducing short quote
; no conjunction
. inside quote
appearance
, conjunction
, parenthetical
affected
; because of comma
, parenthetical
likely
, parenthetical
actually
, series
friendliness

, apposition
valuable
greeting

; illustrative ,
? inside quote

trait
possessed

adage
, introductory

, introductory
success
career

327. Supermarkets

advent
supermarket
, introductory
self-service
, conjunction
, parenthetical
emphasis

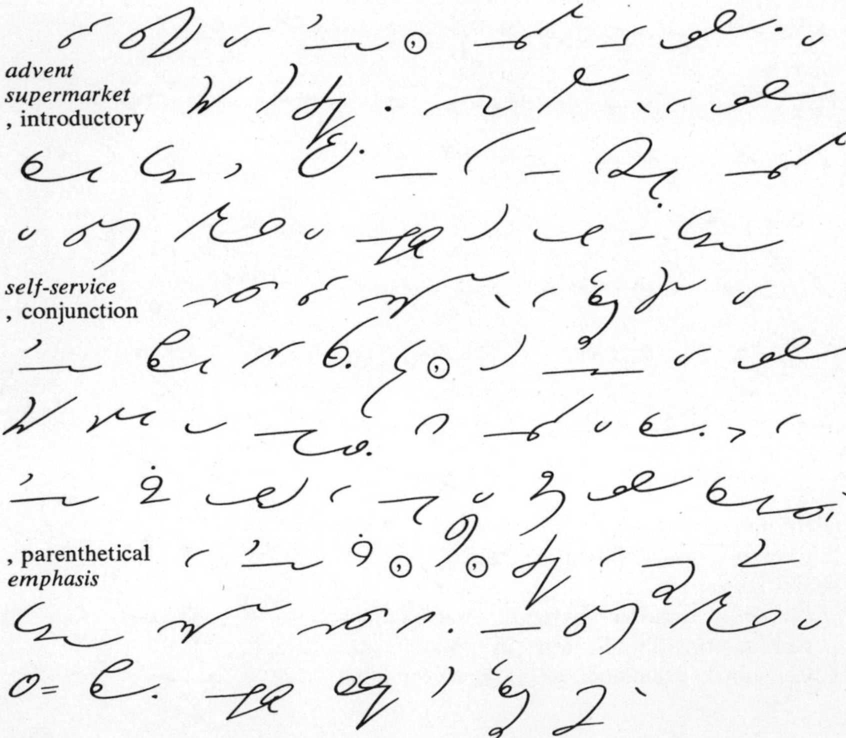

LESSON 46

328. WORD FAMILIES

-MINATE

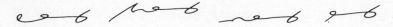

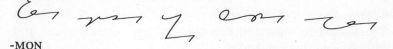

-MENTATION

-MON

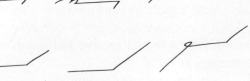

-MINATION

PAST TENSE

Key

Eliminate, discriminate, incriminate, terminate.

Experimentation, instrumentation, regimentation, argumentation, implementation.

Common, summon, sermon, salmon, lemon.

Nomination, illumination, culmination, termination.

Remained, examined, mended, determined.

329. PREVIEW AND WRITING PRACTICE

PREVIEW FOR LETTER **330.**

Key

Tables, shipment, damaged, indicated, extensive.

As soon as, notified, ten-day, enclosed, in order, necessary, information, request.

Will you please, as soon as possible, payment, few days, meantime, another, exactly.

330. Dear Mr. James: You wrote us on November 7 that one of the tables in the shipment you received from us[1] on November 5 was damaged. You indicated that the damage was extensive and that the table was[2] a total loss.

As soon as we received your letter, we notified the Allen Trucking Company, who delivered[3] the merchandise to you. After a ten-day wait, we have received the enclosed form from the Allen Company.[4] In order for them to settle the claim, it will be necessary to have certain information that is requested[5] in this blank. Will you please supply the information and send the form direct to the Allen Company as soon[6] as possible. When the form has been returned, you should receive full payment within a few days for the damaged[7] table.

In the meantime, we are sending you another table exactly like the one that was damaged. Yours[8] truly, (161)

READING AND WRITING PRACTICE

331.

, introducing
short quote

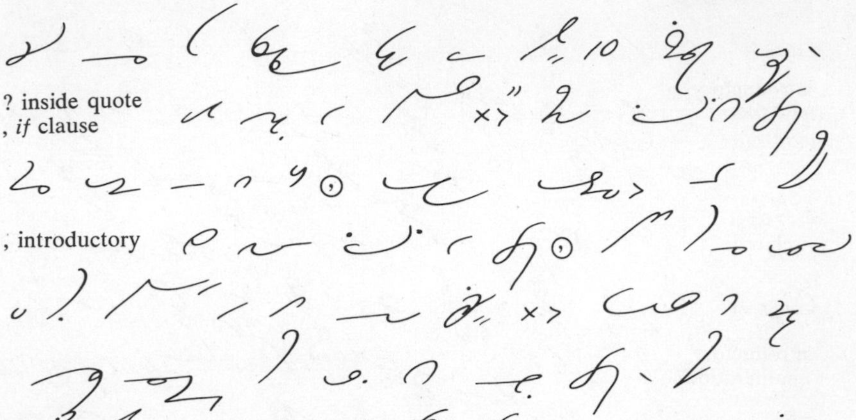

? inside quote
, *if* clause

, introductory

332.

Transcribe:
December 15

, parenthetical
; because of comma
, nonrestrictive

333.

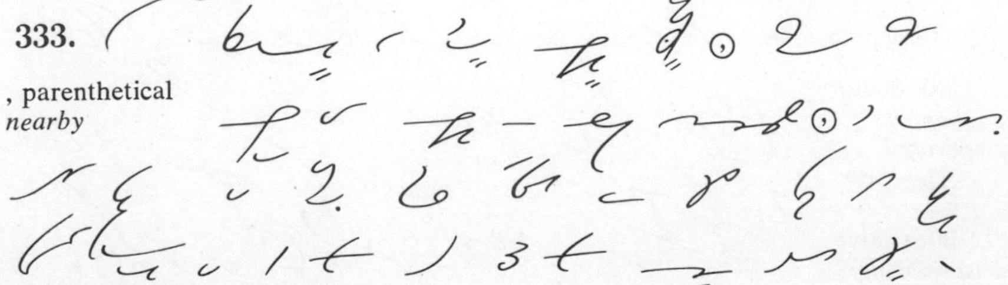

, parenthetical
nearby

CHAPTER X

, introductory
Des Moines
appreciate

successful
, *if* clause

, introductory
: enumeration

accommodations
area
neighborhood

, *if* clause
convenient

334.

, introductory
shoppers
devoted

; illustrative ,
specifically

276

, series
familiar

, apposition
discuss

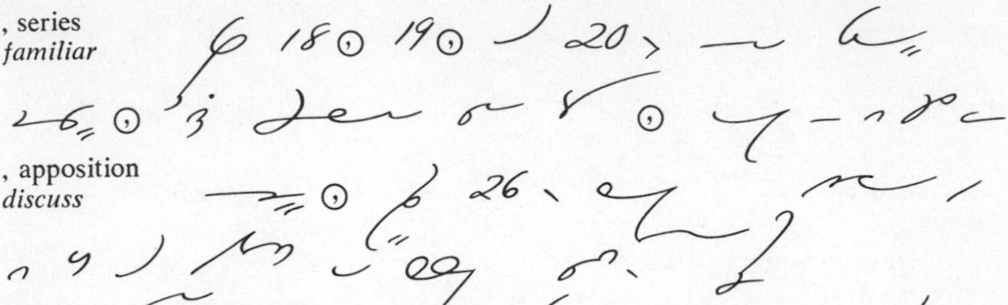

335.

describes
generator
Diesel

passenger
, series

fully qualified
no hyphen
after *ly*

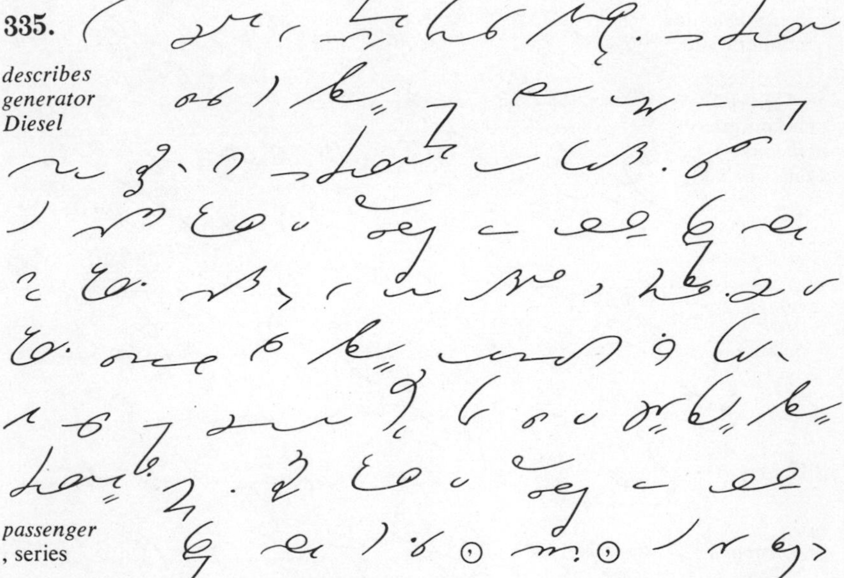

336.

All-Expense
hyphenated
before noun

CHAPTER X

, apposition
, conjunction
amount

accommodations
: enumeration

, *and* omitted
delicious
Louisville's

further
, *if* clause

337.
wheat
Iowa
Minneapolis

. courteous
request

LESSON 47

338. BRIEF-FORM DERIVATIVES

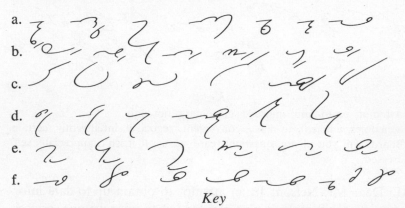

a.

b.

c.

d.

e.

f.

Key

a. Inexperienced, inconsiderate, invaluable, inconclusive, inside, instances, inlet.

b. Allowed, corresponded, enclosed, wondered, referred, regarded.

c. Ended, billed, circled, timed, recognized, parted.

d. Usable, unthinkable, workable, unrecognizable, desirable, valuable.

e. Keeper, purchaser, governor, successor, organizer, writer.

f. Mostly, particularly, rightly, likely, unlikely, instantly, usually, satisfactorily.

339. GEOGRAPHICAL EXPRESSIONS

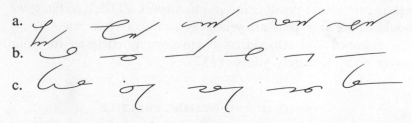

a.

b.

c.

Key

a. Ridgewood, Maplewood, Oakwood, Greenwood, Crestwood.

b. Louisiana, Maine, Maryland, Massachusetts, Michigan, Minnesota.

c. Berlin, Hamburg, Nuremburg, Munich, Bremen.

CHAPTER X

340. PREVIEW AND WRITING PRACTICE

PREVIEW FOR LETTER **341.**

[shorthand characters]

Key

Attempt, up-to-date, improve, customers, not only.

Schedules, efficient, to make, convenient, regularly, intelligently, certain.

Board, will you please, questions, card, to us, if it isn't, appreciate, self-addressed.

341. Dear Mr. Nelson: In an attempt to obtain up-to-date information that will make it possible for us[1] to improve our services, we are asking you and several of our other good customers for help. We not[2] only want our schedules to provide for efficient operation of our trains, but we also want to make[3] them as convenient as possible for those who regularly ride on our trains.

Before we can intelligently[4] improve our services, there are certain facts that we need; namely, where our passengers live and the time they would[5] prefer to board our trains. Therefore, will you please answer the questions on the enclosed card and return it to us. If[6] it isn't possible for you to answer all the questions, we should appreciate your answering as many[7] as you can.

A stamped and self-addressed envelope is enclosed for your convenience. Sincerely yours, (157)

READING AND WRITING PRACTICE

342. *[shorthand characters]*

itineraries
, introductory *[shorthand characters]*

, nonrestrictive
Southern

, parenthetical
copies

343.

, parenthetical
effective

requested
, *as* clause

344.

furniture
, apposition

appreciation
effects

[Shorthand outlines]

, *when* clause
, introducing
    short quote

. inside quote
Company's

barrel
hurry
, parenthetical

345.
: introducing
    long quote
, apposition

, *if* clause
accommodate

. inside quote
, introductory
San Francisco

Furthermore
, introductory

[Shorthand outlines]

, apposition
; because of comma
confused

, *as* clause
previously
schedule

, parenthetical

, *if* clause
contact

346.

, apposition
, nonrestrictive
freight

CHAPTER X

apparently
situation
co-operation

347.

disturbed
, introductory

detailed
, *and* omitted

, series

, introductory
reviewed
adjustments

LESSON 48

348. Useful Business-Letter Phrases

TO

WILL

WOULD

SHOULD

Key

To present, to prepare, to print, to protect, to provide, to brush, to put, to say, to see, to sell.

Will be, will not be, will have, will not have, will be able, will not be able.

Would be, would be able, would be glad, would have, would like, would not, would not be.

Should be, should not, should be able, should be glad, should like, should like to have.

349. Frequent Names

a.

b.

Key

a. Martin, McCarthy, McDonald, McKenzie.

b. Harold, Herbert, Howard, Hugh, Hugo, Isaac, Jacob.

CHAPTER X

350. PREVIEW AND WRITING PRACTICE

PREVIEW FOR LETTER 351.

Key
Carefully, February, damaged, inspected, railroad, therefore.
Occurred, transit, delivery, breakage, accidents, sometimes, handled.
Immediately, complete, as we know, anxious, within, two or three.

351. Dear Mr. West: We were sorry to learn from your letter of March 7 that the carefully packed mirror that we shipped[1] to you on February 27 was damaged when you received it. This mirror was inspected by our[2] Shipping Department before it was sent to the railroad for shipment. The damage, therefore, must have occurred in transit.[3] While our mirrors are well packed to insure delivery without breakage, accidents sometimes happen when the[4] merchandise is handled by the railroad.

If you will return your freight bill, we will place a claim immediately[5] with the local freight office for a complete refund of the purchase price of the mirror.

As we know that you are[6] anxious to have your mirror, we are sending you another one today. It should be delivered to you within[7] two or three days after you receive this letter. Yours very truly, (152)

READING AND WRITING PRACTICE

352.

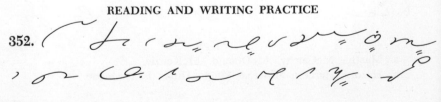

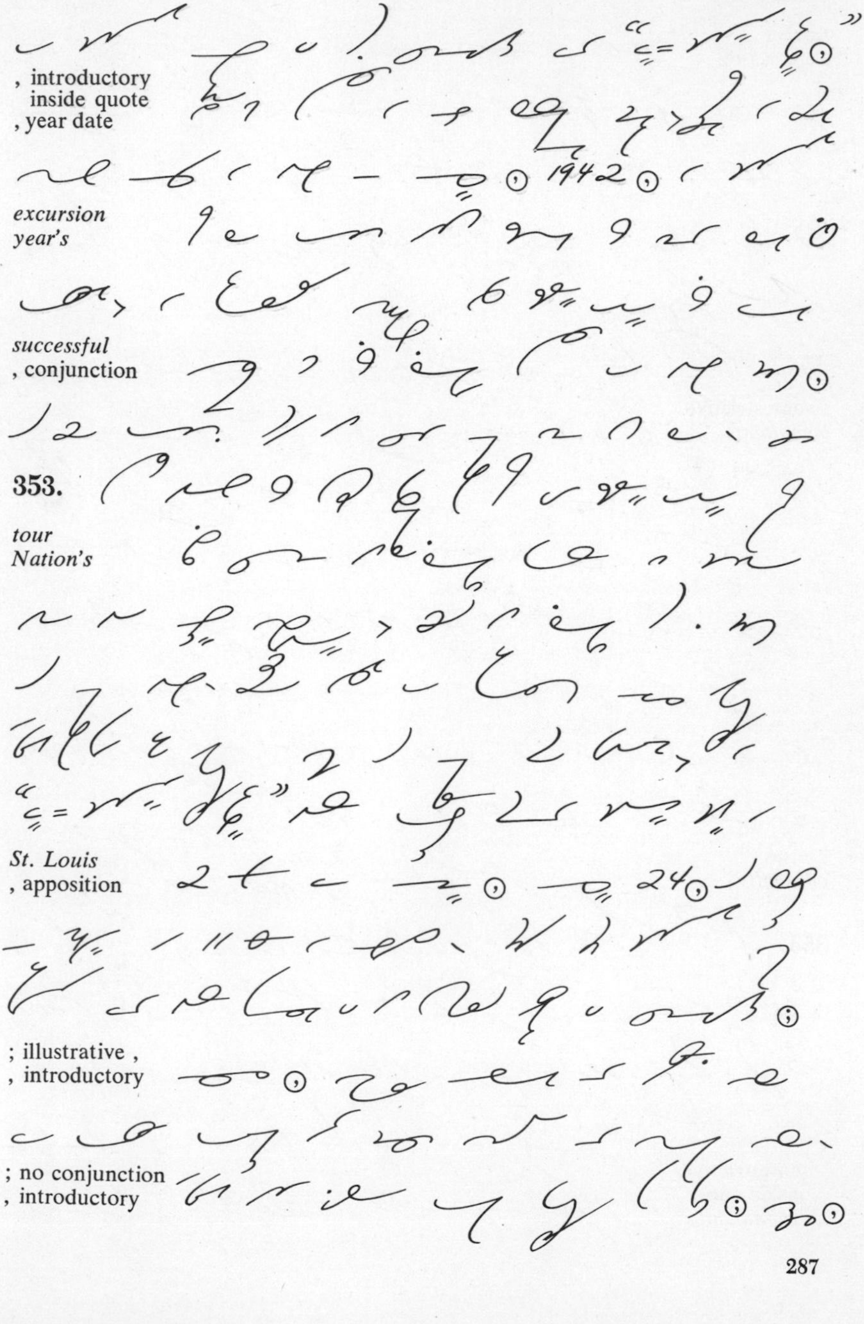

, introductory
inside quote
, year date

excursion
year's

successful
, conjunction

353.

tour
Nation's

St. Louis
, apposition

; illustrative ,
, introductory

; no conjunction
, introductory

further
, apposition

[shorthand]

354.

, nonrestrictive
complaints

[shorthand]

, series
efficiently

355.

[shorthand]

, nonrestrictive
inside quote
accommodates

[shorthand]

seven-day
  hyphenated
  before noun
, *and* omitted

[shorthand outline]

, series
: enumeration

[shorthand outline]

Downing
Eiffel
, series

[shorthand outline]

length
, series

[shorthand outline]

, *as* clause
accommodations

[shorthand outline]

, *if* clause
summer's

[shorthand outline]

356.

round-trip
  hyphenated
  before noun

[shorthand outline]

plane
; no conjunction
, introductory

[shorthand outline]

, *when* clause
unused
, introductory

, nonrestrictive

, introducing
  short quote
, *if* clause
. inside quote

357.

, nonrestrictive
excellent

LESSON 49

358. WORD ENDINGS

-LTY

-RITY

-SHIP

-ULATE

-ULATION

-CAL, -CLE

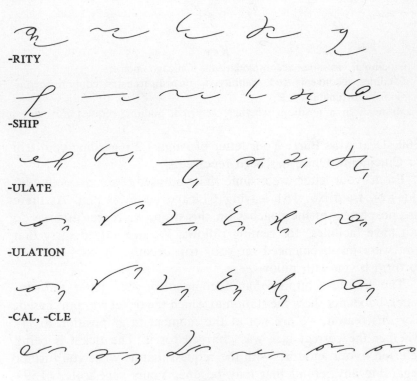

Key

Casualty, cruelty, penalty, faculty, novelty.
Majority, minority, clarity, charity, sincerity, priority.
Relationship, partnership, membership, kinship, worship, championship.
Regulate, stimulate, formulate, speculate, stipulate, granulate.
Regulation, stimulation, formulation, speculation, stipulation, granulation.
Article, chemicals, vertical, chronicle, technical, technically.

CHAPTER X

359. PREVIEW AND WRITING PRACTICE

PREVIEW FOR LETTER 360.

[shorthand symbols]

Key

Cincinnati, assume, accommodations, Chicago, porters.

Facilities, inconvenienced, inability, to furnish, transfer, coupon, accompanied, unfortunately.

Moment, in a position, whether, referred, auditor, request, further.

360. Dear Miss Barr: Your letter of August 2 regarding your trip to Cincinnati, Ohio, has been received.

From[1] your letter, we assume that you used coach accommodations on train No. 161 leaving Chicago at[2] 5:30 p.m. As there are no porters in the coaches on this train, we regret that we do not have facilities[3] for renting pillows. We are indeed sorry that you were inconvenienced on your trip because of our[4] inability to furnish you with pillows.

The transfer coupon that accompanied your letter unfortunately[5] does not show the station at which the ticket was purchased. For this reason, we are not at the moment in a[6] position to say whether the correct fare was charged for it. The ticket is being referred to our auditor,[7] with the request that he write you further regarding any refund that may be due. Yours very truly, (159)

READING AND WRITING PRACTICE

361. *[shorthand symbols]*

Transcribe:
No. 122   *[shorthand symbols]* 122. *[shorthand symbols]*

, introductory

; because of comma

season's
losses

362.

, nonrestrictive
, introducing
  short quote

? inside quote

; because of comma
, *if* clause

volume
, *if* clause
, introductory

CHAPTER X

363.

annual
, apposition

directors
: enumeration

, *if* clause
proxy

, series

364.

up to the minute
no noun,
no hyphen
. courteous
request
; illustrative ,

, parenthetical

believe
, conjunction

, *and* omitted
self-addressed

365.

, introductory
trunk

, introductory
securely
safety

CHAPTER X

, conjunction
anxious

366.

receipt
, introductory

; no conjunction
, introductory
unfortunate

, *when* clause

367.

, introductory
occasion

LESSON 50

368. WORD-BUILDING PRACTICE — EXPRESSION OF *w*

WA

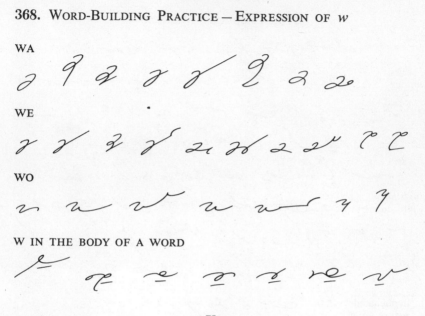

WE

WO

W IN THE BODY OF A WORD

Key

Way, wage, waste, wait, waited, waver, wax, wary.
Wet, weed, west, width, worse, wicked, wing, window, weep, weapon.
Walk, wall, wander, war, warmth, wash, watch.
Dwell, equip, queer, quick, quit, square, quarter.

369. ACCURACY PRACTICE — OO HOOK

a.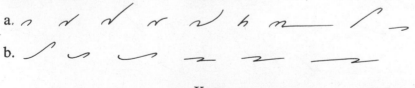

b.

Key

a. You, yours truly, you would, other, you want, shoe, woman, do, knew.
b. Into, are you, will you, noon, number, monument.

READING AND WRITING PRACTICE

370. Telephone Manners

, series
unions

invisible
, introductory

New York's
best-known
hyphenated
before noun

, series
grudgingly

, series
employee's

, parenthetical
courtesy

pleasant
offering

, series
exercises

, conjunction
, series

, introducing
   short quote
, introductory
   inside quote

CHAPTER X

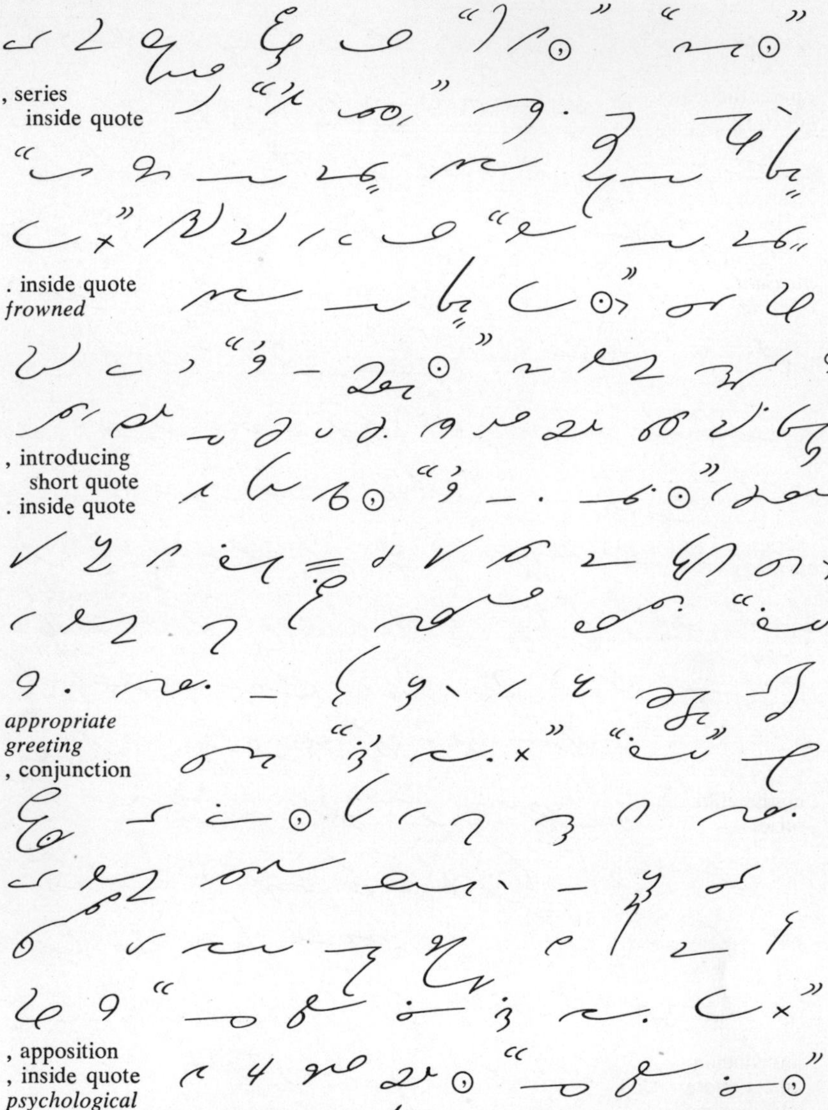
, series
inside quote
. inside quote
frowned
, introducing
short quote
. inside quote
appropriate
greeting
, conjunction
, apposition
, inside quote
psychological

, introductory

: introducing
   long quote
, conjunction

. inside quote

, *when* clause
frequently
transferred

System's
operators
courteous

supervisor
chief
, series

CHAPTER X

voice-recording
  hyphenated
  before noun
discs

, series
girl's

, introductory

, inside quote
Already

[shorthand]

—Don Wharton

CHAPTER **XI**

LESSON 51

371. WORD FAMILIES

-DENCE, -DENSE

-DOM

-TAIN

-TANCE

-TENT

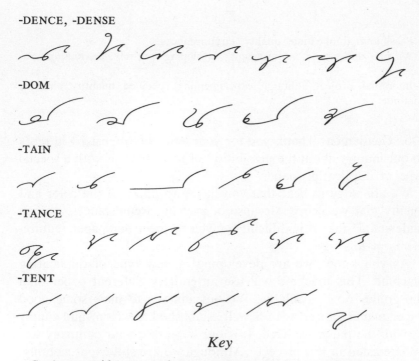

Key

Credence, evidence, prudence, condense, residence, coincidence, providence.

Random, kingdom, freedom, seldom, wisdom.

Contain, retain, maintain, detain, certain, obtain.

Acceptance, substance, distance, admittance, circumstance, circumstances.

Intent, content, patent, extent, discontent, competent.

CHAPTER XI

372. PREVIEW AND WRITING PRACTICE

PREVIEW FOR LETTER **373.**

Key

Possibility, duplicating, quality, circumstances.

We can understand, requirement, developing, entirely, anxious, manufacturer.

Interested, project, although, experimenting, specified, quantity, amount, continue.

373. Gentlemen: Thank you for your letter of August 14 in reply to our inquiry about the possibility[1] of furnishing us with a special type of duplicating paper.

We are sorry to hear that you have[2] no paper of the color and quality that we desire. Because of present circumstances, we can understand[3] that it is difficult for you to meet our paper requirements at this time.

As you know, we are developing[4] a new type of duplicating machine. This machine will use an entirely different paper than the grades now[5] available. We are anxious to have some good paper manufacturer, who is well established, develop[6] and supply us with the paper we need. It is our hope that your company will be interested in this project.[7] Although we are still experimenting, the paper that we specified seems to work best.

Even though you cannot[8] supply us with this paper in quantity at the present time, could you send us a limited amount so[9] that we could continue our testing?

May we hear from you by return mail. Yours very truly, (196)

READING AND WRITING PRACTICE

374.

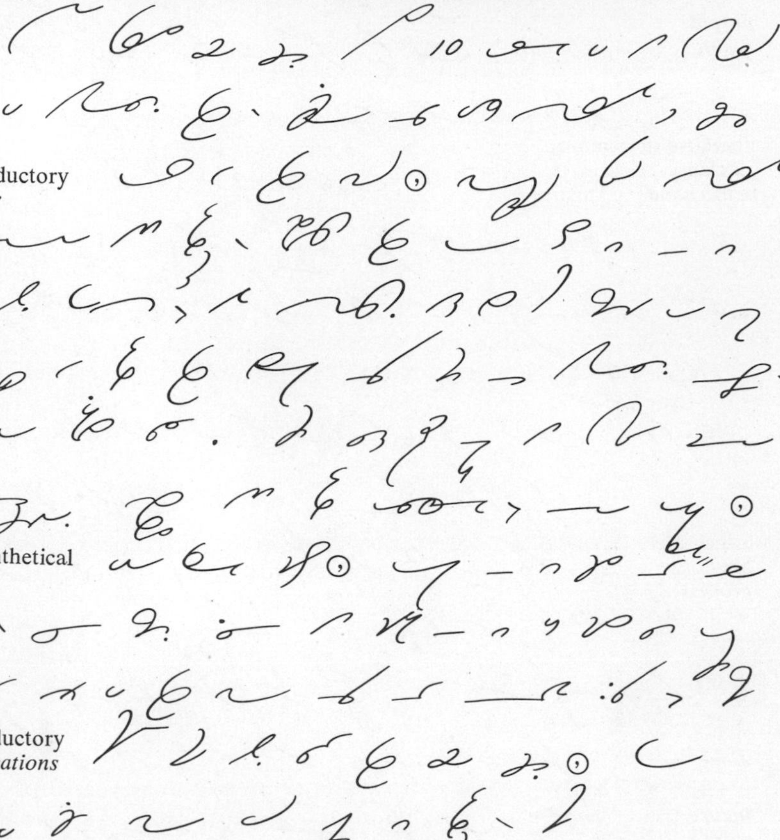

, introductory
similar

, parenthetical
sales

, introductory
specifications

375.

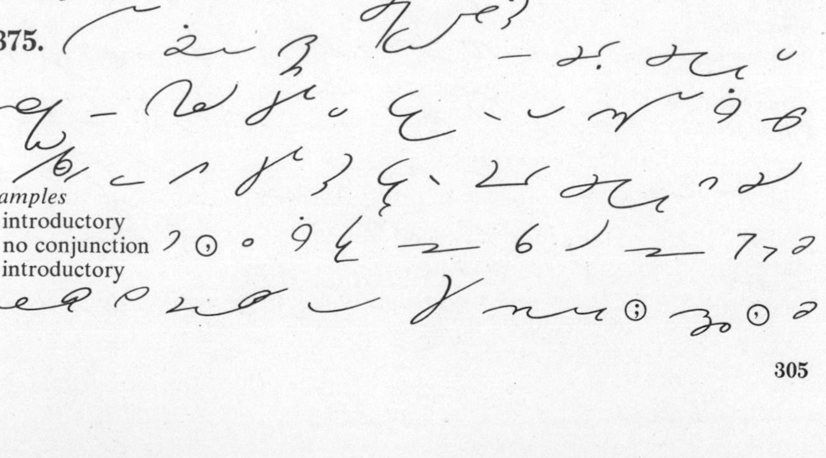

samples
, introductory
; no conjunction
, introductory

purple
fading

; because of comma
, if clause
beforehand

376.

, as clause
previous
processes

induce
store's
wrapping

, nonrestrictive
personnel

statistical
; illustrative ,

(shorthand outlines)

377.

accepted
co-operative

, parenthetical
mutually

, introductory
: enumeration
point-of-sale
hyphenated
before noun
, series

, *and* omitted
durable

378.

CHAPTER XI

, introducing
  short quote
. inside quote

[shorthand outlines]

, year date
companies

1952

[shorthand outlines]

northern
, apposition
, *if* clause

copies
Duluth

[shorthand outlines]

379.
Transcribe:
  No. 140
  July 2.

[shorthand outlines]

, introductory

[shorthand outlines]

LESSON 52

380. BRIEF-FORM DERIVATIVES

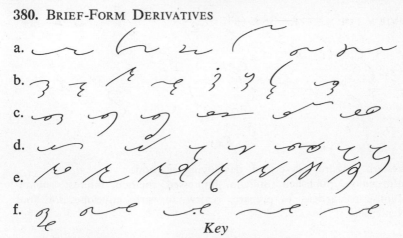

Key

a. Longer, bigger, sooner, timer, weaker, circular.

b. Considers, instances, desires, corresponds, houses, offices, businesses, requests.

c. Reconsider, recover, recovery, renumber, redirect, rewrite.

d. Reorganize, reorder, republic, restate, reunite, represent, representative.

e. Disregard, dispel, dislike, disbelieve, disorder, dissatisfaction, disadvantage.

f. Usefulness, uselessness, willingness, gladness, greatness.

381. GEOGRAPHICAL EXPRESSIONS

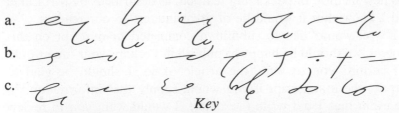

Key

a. Marlborough, Jonesboro, Hillsboro, Attleboro, Goldsboro.

b. Mississippi, Missouri, Montana, Nebraska, Nevada, New Hampshire, New Jersey, New Mexico.

c. Naples, Rome, Sicily, Budapest, Vienna, Prague.

CHAPTER XI

382. PREVIEW AND WRITING PRACTICE

PREVIEW FOR LETTER **383.**

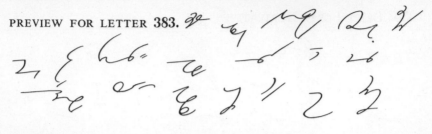

Key

Western, research, described, developing, seafood.
Information, published, Bulletin, impressed, method, interest, submit.
Manuscript, article, to prepare, review, forward, envelope, for your convenience.

383. Dear Mr. Smith: On Monday, October 7, I attended a meeting of the Western Association[1] of Food Packers. At this meeting I heard a report given by Mr. Lake, of your research department, in which[2] he described a new process you are developing for the packaging of seafood.

Is this process well enough[3] developed so that you could give me information for an article to be published in an early issue[4] of the Food Packers Bulletin? I was very much impressed with this new method of packaging seafood, as described[5] by Mr. Lake; and I know that it would be of great interest to our readers.

If you would like to submit[6] a completed manuscript on this process, we should be happy to publish it. Perhaps your time would not permit[7] you to write the article. If so, I should be glad to prepare the manuscript if you would supply the[8] information. In the event that I did write the article, I would want you to review it before it was published.[9]

I shall look forward to hearing from you soon. A stamped envelope is enclosed for your convenience. Yours very truly,[10] (200)

READING AND WRITING PRACTICE

384.

technical
article
Lake's

development
laboratory

, as clause
, and omitted
reliable

(*, parenthetical*
Scientific

; no conjunction
, parenthetical
rewarding

worth while
no noun,
no hyphen

, conjunction

385.

, series
absorption

, *when* clause
primarily
physical

; illustrative ,
, series
legal

, *if* clause
further
assistance

386.

(shorthand outlines)

, parenthetical
durability

Transcribe:
100 per cent

permanence
, introductory

, introductory
, introducing
   short quote
Price's
. inside quote

387.

, nonrestrictive
August's

follow-up
hyphenated
before noun

, introductory
schedules

, *if* clause
; no conjunction
substitutions

388.

, introductory
: enumeration
, series

, *when* clause

389.

, introductory
processes

LESSON 53

390. Useful Business-Letter Phrases

AGO

WANT

IS NOT, WAS NOT

BEEN

Key

Days ago, few days ago, months ago, few months ago, weeks ago.

I want, we want, you want, they want, he wants, who wants, they wanted, if you wanted.

There is not, there isn't, if it is not, if it isn't, he was not, he wasn't, I wasn't, it was not.

Have been, have not been, I have been, I have not been, we have been, we have not been, has not been, there has been, had been, would have been.

391. Frequent Names

a.

b.

Key

a. Miller, Mitchell, Moore, Morgan.
b. Hortense, Ida, Irene, Jean, Jeannette, Josephine, Judith, Julia.

315

CHAPTER XI

392. PREVIEW AND WRITING PRACTICE

PREVIEW FOR LETTER **393.**

PREVIEW FOR LETTER **394.**

Key
Requested, specifications, proposing, results, requirements.
100 per cent, entirely, standards, chemical, qualified, technical, assist.
10,000, duplicate, exactly, sample.
Color, agency, our understanding, you did, purchase, separately.

393. Dear Mr. Field: As you requested in your letter of February 8, our research staff has checked carefully the[1] specifications for the grades of paper you are proposing to use.

The results of these tests show that the requirements[2] for 100 per cent rag, 50 per cent rag, and 25 per cent rag, respectively,[3] are entirely in line with what we consider to be good standards for these grades.

As we do not make a chemical[4] wood grade paper, we are not qualified to give an opinion on that grade. If you would like to have our Technical[5] Department do any further testing for you, we should be happy to assist you. Yours very truly,[6]

394. Dear Sir: We should like to obtain a rerun of 10,000 copies of the attached catalogue page. The rerun[7] should duplicate exactly the enclosed sample in size and color.

The catalogue was developed by the Dale[8] Agency, and it is our understanding that you did the printing of this catalogue for the Dale Agency.[9]

A purchase order will be sent to you separately by our Purchasing Department. Yours very truly,[10] (200)

READING AND WRITING PRACTICE

395.
reams
Transcribe:
April 1

, introductory
accept

, parenthetical

absorb
, introductory

396.

, introducing
short quote
. inside quote

, introductory

397.
, parenthetical
effective
medium

well-established
hyphenated
before noun

, *if* clause
specialty
, conjunction

398.
Transcribe
No. 2156
50 per cent

; illustrative ,

facilitate
, introductory

399.
, apposition
parcel
cartons

Whiteline's
quality
, and omitted

, when clause
, parenthetical
ideally

steadily increasing
no hyphen
after ly

CHAPTER XI

if clause
samples

400.

, nonrestrictive
, year date
February

1908

, *if* clause

401.

50,

hundredweight
policy
advance

32^{18}

acceptable
. *courteous*
 request

LESSON 54

402. WORD BEGINNINGS

SHORT-

SUPER-

TRANS-

OVER-

UNDER-

INTR-

Key

Short, shortest, shortly, shorter, shortened, shortsighted, shortcomings, shortage, shortcake.

Superhuman, superintend, supervise, supervised, supervisory, supervision, supernatural.

Transmit, transform, transplant, transit, transpire, transatlantic.

Overturn, overplay, overcome, overcoat, oversupply, overheated.

Underneath, underline, undersell, undersigned, understudy, understatement.

Introduce, introduced, introduction, intrude, introvert, intrigue, intricate.

CHAPTER XI

403. Preview and Writing Practice

PREVIEW FOR LETTER **404.**

Key

Beautiful, attractive, stationery, comparable, regardless.
Create, quality, letterhead, evaluate, measuring, standards.
You would like to have, submit, suitable, obligation, interest, to purchase, card.

404. Dear Mr. Burns: I am sure you have a beautiful office that is well equipped with fine furniture and the latest[1] machines. You probably have in your employ well-dressed salesmen and attractive, well-groomed office workers.

Is your[2] office stationery, however, comparable in attractiveness to the furniture, machines, and people[3] in your office? Regardless of how well a letter is typed, it will not create the most favorable impression[4] if it appears on poor-quality stationery. If you are in doubt about the quality of your letterhead,[5] please send a sample to us; we shall be glad to evaluate it for you.

Should our tests show that your letterhead[6] is not measuring up to the high standards we think you would like to have, we shall be glad to submit samples of[7] the type of office stationery that we feel would be suitable for your business. There is no charge or obligation[8] for this service. If you find it to your interest to purchase our high-quality letterhead paper,[9] you will be amazed at the low cost.

Please return the enclosed card so that we may know of your interest. Yours[10] truly, (201)

READING AND WRITING PRACTICE

405.

tissue
Manila
, series

, introductory
category

; illustrative ,
manufacture

, conjunction
appreciate

406.

, introductory
, introducing
   short quote

. inside quote
acquaint

, introductory
realization

present-day
   hyphenated
   before noun

[Shorthand text with margin annotations]

, nonrestrictive
: introducing
    long quote

excellent

. inside quote

, introductory
, parenthetical

, introductory

407.

, introductory
cellophane

, year date
undoubtedly

(shorthand outlines)

; because of comma
, *as* clause

, *if* clause

408.

, *as* clause
; series

well-arranged
hyphenated
before noun
neatly typed
no hyphen
after *ly*

, introductory
variety

CHAPTER XI

, introducing
   short quote
. inside quote

409.

weight
analyzed
, parenthetical

over-all
   hyphenated
   before noun
, introductory

dissatisfaction
, conjunction
, *if* clause

410.

, apposition
strength

possibility
, *as* clause

, introductory

LESSON 55

411. WORD-BUILDING PRACTICE — BLENDS

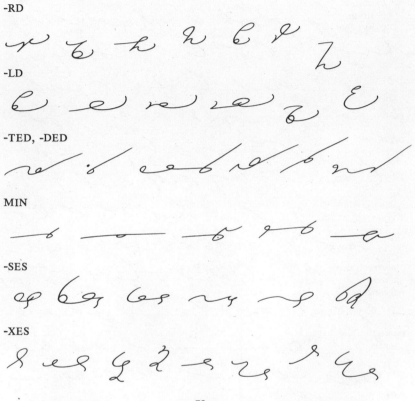

-RD

-LD

-TED, -DED

MIN

-SES

-XES

Key

Restored, repaired, measured, assured, appeared, stared, injured.
Appealed, mailed, skilled, smiled, compiled, expelled.
Greeted, heated, eliminated, traded, deeded, excluded.
Minute, minimum, miniature, terminate, minister.
Arises, balances, premises, closes, glasses, advises.
Taxes, relaxes, prefixes, suffixes, mixes, reflexes, indexes, perplexes.

CHAPTER XI

READING AND WRITING PRACTICE

412. The Business Letter and Collections

up to date
no noun,
no hyphen

overdue
success

, nonrestrictive
varying
necessitate

implies
, series

latter
, series

, parenthetical
response

, when clause
effective

; because of comma
, when clause

, parenthetical
embarrass

413. The Business Letter and Adjustments

discourteous
, series

grievances
, parenthetical

adjustment
; because of comma
, parenthetical

, parenthetical

, *when* clause
perspective
, parenthetical

angered
customer's

414. The Sales Letter

, introductory
media

first-class
  hyphenated
  before noun

emphasized
preferred

circulars
, series

costly
, introductory

conviction
. inside quote

degree
showmanship

Certainly
; no conjunction

, introductory
dramatic

CHAPTER XI

arouse
novel

, parenthetical
man's

, parenthetical
razor

, if clause
, parenthetical
objective

LESSON 56

415. WORD FAMILIES

-LUTION

-NCTION

-TIONER

-IZATION

-DUCTION

Key

Solution, resolution, revolution, dissolution, evolution, allusion.
Function, junction, extinction, injunction, conjunction, sanction.
Commissioner, practitioner, stationer, questioner, pensioner, petitioner.
Authorization, naturalization, civilization, nationalization, centralization.
Deduction, reduction, production, introduction, reproduction, induction.

CHAPTER XII

416. PREVIEW AND WRITING PRACTICE

PREVIEW FOR LETTER **417.**

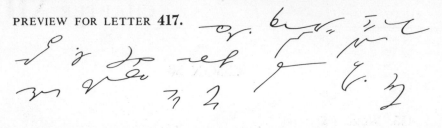

Key

My understanding, Charleston, interested, will you please.
In order that, whether, family's, in relation to the, downtown, district.
Construction, I should like to know, insulation, to furnish, determine, obtaining, for your convenience.

417. Dear Sir: It is my understanding that your house, which is located in Charleston, will soon be for sale. I am opening[1] a branch office in Charleston in the very near future, and I am interested in buying a house[2] there.

Will you please give me the following information about your house in order that I may know whether it[3] will meet my family's needs: (1) Where is it located in relation to the downtown section? (2) How far is[4] it from a public school? (3) Is there a shopping district within a short distance of the house? (4) How many rooms does[5] it have and what is the type of construction? (5) In addition, I should like to know the model of the furnace[6] in the house, the extent of insulation, and the size of the lot.

If you will be kind enough to furnish me[7] with this information, together with the price you are asking, I shall then be able to determine whether[8] your house will meet our needs.

As I must take some action immediately about obtaining a house, I hope you[9] will be able to send me this information without delay. A stamped envelope is enclosed for your convenience.[10] Yours truly, (202)

READING AND WRITING PRACTICE

418.

, introductory
; because of comma;
delighted

elementary
senior
, conjunction

, conjunction

, series
wood-burning
hyphenated
before noun

, conjunction

, *and* omitted

[shorthand outlines]

4702

15=

13

, nonrestrictive
landscaped

, 80,   150,

, *if* clause

realtor
, conjunction

419.

description
, apposition

20 × 9   10:30

, introductory
forward

420.

Senator
, *as* clause

, *when* clause
legislature

, introducing
short quote
. inside quote

, introductory
; illustrative ,
, series

surf
taught
, series

feasible
necessity
, parenthetical

e .

421.

; no conjunction
gratified

worth-while
hyphenated
before noun

; no conjunction
, and omitted
natural

5

supplies
reasonably

LESSON 57

422. BRIEF-FORM DERIVATIVES

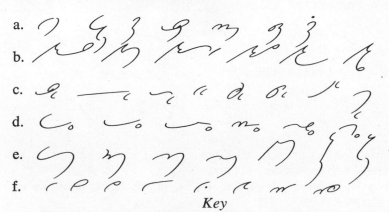

a.

b.

c.

d.

e.

f.

Key

a. Thankful, purposeful, wishful, rightful, wonderful, useful, houseful.

b. Dislike, discover, disorganized, disorderly, displease, disbelieve.

c. Writings, mornings, workings, things, sidings, outings, endings, coverings.

d. Pleasingly, willingly, longingly, wonderingly, correspondingly, questioningly.

e. Progressive, successive, conclusive, corrective, directive, subjective, objective.

f. The, that, they, them, think, those, worth, otherwise.

423. GEOGRAPHICAL EXPRESSIONS

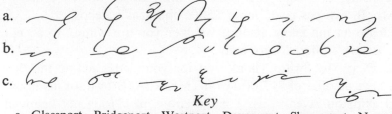

a.

b.

c.

Key

a. Glassport, Bridgeport, Westport, Davenport, Shreveport, Newport, Gulfport.

b. New York, North Carolina, North Dakota, Ohio, Oklahoma, Oregon, Pennsylvania, South Carolina.

c. Bucharest, Athens, Moscow, Oslo, Stockholm, Copenhagen.

339

CHAPTER XII

424. PREVIEW AND WRITING PRACTICE

PREVIEW FOR LETTER **425.**

PREVIEW FOR LETTER **426.**

Key

To know, Lexington, liked, $17,000.

Very good, situation, I hope you will be, to sell, figure, please let us know, accept.

Thank you for your letter, desirous, financial, dealings.

As you know, Toledo, consequently, urgent, complete, transaction.

---

425. Dear Mr. Jackson: You will be happy to know that early this morning we showed your house at 1021 Lexington[1] Avenue to Mr. and Mrs. R. A. Brown. Both Mr. and Mrs. Brown liked the house very much and[2] have made an offer of $17,000.

While you have listed the house at $18,000, I[3] feel that this offer of $17,000 is very good when the present market situation is[4] considered. I hope you will be willing to sell at this figure.

Mr. Brown has given me a $500[5] check as a deposit.

Please let me know at once whether you are willing to accept Mr. Brown's offer. Yours truly,[6]

426. Dear Mr. Swift: Thank you for your letter telling me that you have an offer of $17,000 from[7] Mr. R. A. Brown for my house on Lexington Avenue. As I am desirous of closing my financial dealings[8] here in the city, I am willing to accept the $17,000 offer.

As you know, I have[9] to be in Toledo by the first of the month; consequently, it is urgent that I complete the details of[10] the transaction before I leave. Yours truly, (207)

READING AND WRITING PRACTICE

427.

, parenthetical
first-floor
  hyphenated
  before noun

890

adjustment
, conjunction

, *as* clause
; because of
  comma

, *as* clause

428.

1109

: enumeration
gauge

, *as* clause
, nonrestrictive
thermostat

; illustrative,
furnace

, introductory
, series
ideal

429.

, introductory
, year date
, introductory

desirable
, parenthetical

(shorthand outlines)

, introductory
arrangements

, parenthetical
appreciation

, apposition
, introducing
  short quote

. inside quote
neighbor

, apposition
, inside quote

430.
badly needed
no hyphen
after *ly*

, *as* clause
worn

CHAPTER XII

, *and* omitted
efficient
economical

, introductory
eaves

, *when* clause
rainfall

431.

, parenthetical
troughs

, parenthetical
, introductory
immediately

344

LESSON 58

432. Useful Business-Letter Phrases

OF COURSE

WE HOPE

I HOPE

LET US

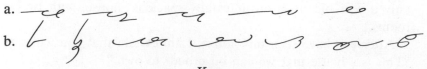

Key

Of course, of course it is, of course it is not, of course it will, of course it will be.

We hope, we hope that, we hope that the, we hope that this, we hope you can, we hope you will, we hope you are.

I hope, I hope the, I hope that, I hope that this, I hope you are, I hope you can, I hope you will, I hope you have.

Let us, let us see, let us have, please let us, please let us have.

433. Frequent Names

a.

b.

Key
a. Morris, Morrison, Morse, Monroe, Murray.
b. John, Joseph, Lawrence, Leonard, Louis, Michael, Nathan.

CHAPTER XII

434. PREVIEW AND WRITING PRACTICE

PREVIEW FOR LETTER **435.**

Key

Representative, short time ago, appreciated, qualified, thoroughly understands.

Has been, successful, houses, establishments, inspected, properties, interested, to find.

Milford, newest, unusually, spacious, proud, why not, appointment.

435. Dear Mr. James: The consideration you gave Mr. G. R. Meyers, our representative, when he called on[1] you a short time ago is appreciated.

Mr. Meyers is well qualified to advise you on real[2] estate matters, as he thoroughly understands all phases of the business. Mr. Meyers has been with our company[3] for over ten years, and he has been most successful in selling all types of houses and business establishments.[4]

Yesterday morning he inspected the two properties that you listed with our company, and at the[5] present time he is showing both properties to interested parties.

As you requested him to find you a[6] desirable house in this city, I should like to suggest a house that has just become available in Milford[7] Heights. This is the newest house we have listed, being only a year old. It is an unusually spacious[8] house, with twelve rooms.

After you have seen this house, I am certain that you will say, "This is a house that we can be proud[9] to own."

Mr. Meyers will be happy to show you this house. Why not call him and make an appointment. Yours very truly,[10] (200)

READING AND WRITING PRACTICE

436.

Sunday's
property

County
, apposition

two-story
hyphenated
before noun

, as clause
already
historically

acreage
, nonrestrictive

, year date

: enumeration
, conjunction
insulated

[shorthand outlines]

; because of comma
, apposition

437.

description
, introductory

landmarks
, as clause

, introductory
, apposition

, *if* clause

438.
reputed
reliable
, as clause

[Shorthand outlines]

anxious
, introductory
; because of comma

Transcribe:
$10,000

439.

: enumeration
5-acre
   hyphenated
   before noun
, series

semimodern

(shorthand symbols)

; because of comma
, introductory

(shorthand symbols)

, introductory

440.

, *as* clause
; because of comma
preference

mind
, *when* clause

, conjunction
Saturday

LESSON 59

441. WORD ENDINGS

-WARD

-TAIN

-CIENT, -CIENCY

-OR, -ER

-TUAL

-URE

Key

Backward, forward, onward, inward, outward, westward, southward.

Entertain, obtain, certain, fountain, pertain, detain, maintain.

Deficient, proficient, efficient, inefficient, patient, proficiency, efficiency, deficiency.

Writer, contributor, distributor, shipper, director, organizer.

Actual, mutual, factual, actually, mutually.

Secure, secured, insecure, procure, procured, failure, tenure.

351

CHAPTER XII

442. PREVIEW AND WRITING PRACTICE

PREVIEW FOR LETTER **443.**

Key

Thank you for your letter, ideal, includes, third; 10,000; square feet.
100 feet, in addition, private, specific, accommodations, interest, refinished, artificial.
Entire, comfort, elevator, stairway, indeed, firsthand, facilities.

443. Gentlemen: Thank you for your letter of June 7, in which you inquire about the space that we have available[1] in the Masey Building. This space should prove ideal for a dancing school such as yours. It includes the entire third floor,[2] containing more than 10,000 square feet of floor space. The large hall is 100 feet long and 50 feet wide. In[3] addition, there are several small rooms that would be excellent for private lessons. The large hall could be used to[4] good advantage for the dancing classes. It would also be excellent as a ballroom for parties.

Here are a[5] few specific details concerning the accommodations that should be of interest to you:

1. The floors have[6] been refinished recently.

2. The rooms are well lighted, with both natural and artificial lighting.

3. The[7] entire building is air conditioned for year-round comfort.

4. There is elevator service to the third floor as[8] well as a large stairway.

We should be happy, indeed, to show you this space in the Masey Building so that you could[9] see at firsthand the facilities available for your dancing school.

May we hear from you soon. Yours truly,[10] (200)

READING AND WRITING PRACTICE

444.

, nonrestrictive
historical

, *and* omitted
modern

, *as* clause
quiet

, nonrestrictive
pamphlets

445.

, parenthetical
pleasant

, introductory
, apposition

CHAPTER XII

: introducing
  long quote
, *if* clause

, conjunction
neighborhood

. inside quote

, year date
, *if* clause

1953

446.
, apposition
, introducing
  short quote
. inside quote

, introductory
, nonrestrictive

120

; no conjunction
, introductory

[Gregg shorthand outlines]

, series
utensils

, apposition
, *as* clause

, parenthetical
similar

, nonrestrictive
utilities

, *if* clause
, introductory
, parenthetical

447.

CHAPTER XII

[shorthand]

; illustrative ,
, series
, introductory

[shorthand]

, *when* clause

[shorthand]

448.
excellent
recommendations
, introductory

[shorthand]

, introductory
; because of comma

[shorthand]

, series

[shorthand]

LESSON 60

449. WORD-BUILDING PRACTICE — OMISSION OF VOWELS

OMISSION OF SHORT U

OMISSION OF OW

OMISSION OF E IN DIPHTHONG U

OMISSION OF MINOR VOWEL

Key

Touch, lunch, smudge, much, fund, refund, clutch, judge.
Town, down, around, surround, brown, county, crown, gown.
Avenue, continue, induce, inducement, introduce, produce, suit, revenue.
Millions, radius, miscellaneous, courteous, graduate.

450. ACCURACY PRACTICE — CURVES

a.

b.

Key

a. Present, please, brain, blame, free, value.
b. Pay, bay, see, fee, very, about, as, half, advantage, he is, if, ever.

READING AND WRITING PRACTICE

451. Rolling Homes Gather No Mortgages

[Shorthand outlines]

trailer
Transcribe:
  93 per cent

vacationers
, nonrestrictive

, parenthetical
Curtiss

; because of comma
, series

. inside quote

[Shorthand outlines]

, introductory
breaking

conveyance
, parenthetical

garage
, series

, year date

, conjunction

popular
flimsy
, apposition

; because of comma
, parenthetical
pioneer

, parenthetical

varieties
, series
, parenthetical

, parenthetical

, introductory

, parenthetical

newly married
  no hyphen
  after *ly*
, parenthetical

, introductory
; because of comma

, series

built-in
  hyphenated
  before noun

well-planned
   hyphenated
   before noun

, series
recreation
, introductory

: enumeration
, nonrestrictive
thousands

, introductory
, introducing
  short quote
. inside quote

CHAPTER XIII

LESSON 61

452. WORD FAMILIES

-CATE

-GATE

-IETY

-QUENT

-OLOGY

Key

Complicate, educate, abdicate, indicate, certificate, allocate.
Delegate, investigate, interrogate, instigate, obligate.
Society, variety, propriety, sobriety, anxiety, notoriety, dubiety.
Frequent, subsequent, consequent, delinquent, eloquent, infrequent.
Psychology, technology, apology, analogy, bacteriology.

CHAPTER XIII

453. PREVIEW AND WRITING PRACTICE

PREVIEW FOR LETTER **454.**

PREVIEW FOR LETTER **455.**

Key
Something, carbon, vision, disposition, formula.
Clarity, features, economical, separate, envelope, sending you, next.
Impression, stencils, bulletins, unbeatable.
Duplicating, sensitive, plastic, uniformly, maximum, variety.

454. Dear Mr. Allen: Here is something new—a carbon copy that is a pleasure to read. When you use Wilson's[1] carbon paper, you save your vision, time, and disposition. This carbon paper is made by a formula that[2] assures clarity and eye appeal even to the last of many copies.

Another feature you will like about[3] Wilson's carbon paper is that it is economical to use; that is, you will get more good copies from each[4] sheet.

In a separate envelope we are sending you several sheets of this new carbon paper. After you[5] have used these samples, we know that you will say, "Please send us Wilson's carbon paper on our next order." Yours truly,[6]

455. Dear Mr. Young: You will always make a good impression when you bring Burns stencils and inks into play on your sales[7] bulletins and office forms. You will find that these stencils and inks make an unbeatable team.

Each stencil duplicating[8] job "comes alive" when it is run on a Burns stencil. The sensitive plastic coat of the stencil makes copy[9] after copy so uniformly clear that it resembles top-quality printing.

Experience has shown,[10] too, that this stencil will give you much longer runs, thus saving time lost in retyping.

Burns duplicator inks yield[11] the maximum number of clear sharp copies from each stencil; and you can obtain these inks in a wide variety[12] of attractive colors.

Mail the enclosed coupon today for a free folder of samples. Yours very truly,[13] (260)

READING AND WRITING PRACTICE

456.

, series
, introductory
executives

: enumeration
men's

accomplishment
subordinates
confusion

, nonrestrictive
, year date
attractive

1936

, conjunction
ideas
, *as* clause

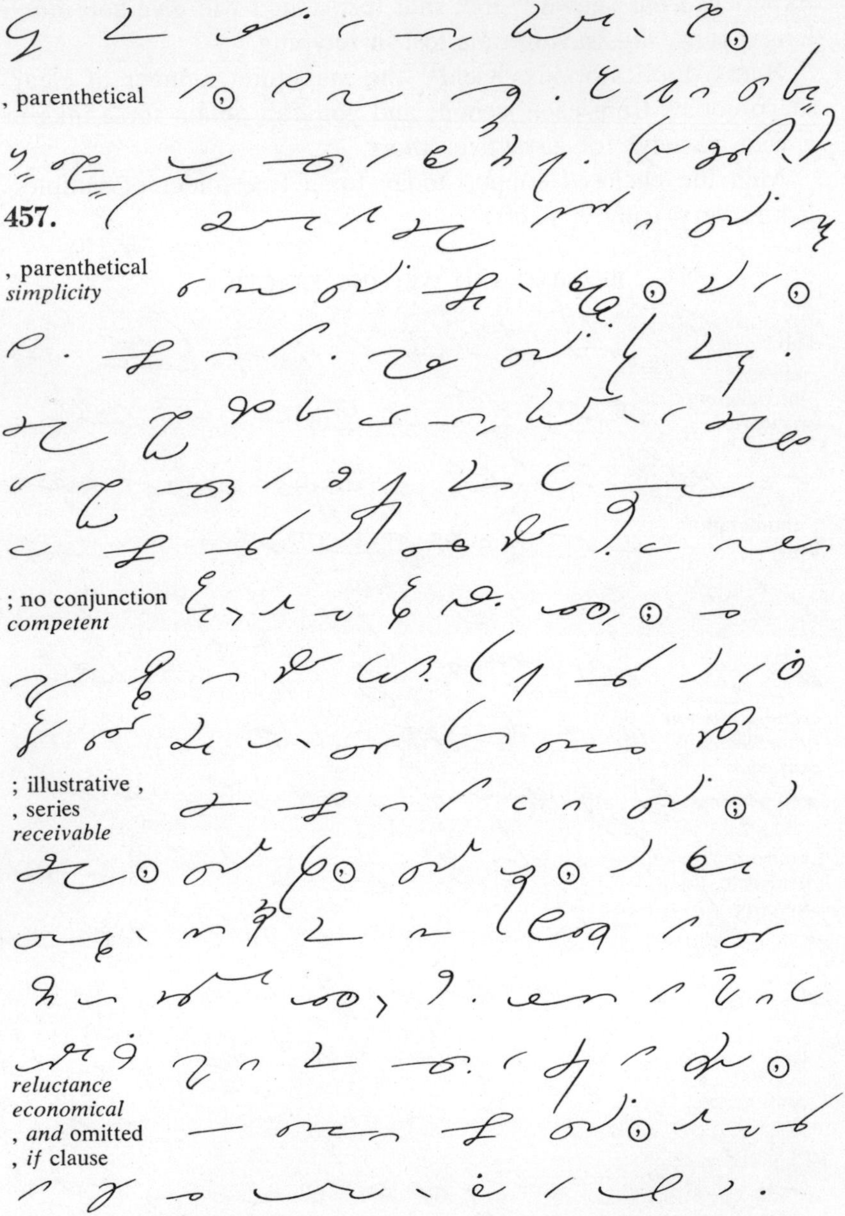

, parenthetical

457.

, parenthetical
simplicity

; no conjunction
competent

; illustrative ,
, series
receivable

reluctance
economical
, *and* omitted
, *if* clause

adjusted
, parenthetical
; no conjunction

[shorthand outlines]

, apposition
widely used
  no hyphen
  after *ly*

458.

announce
internal
medium

[shorthand outlines]

: enumeration

[shorthand outlines]

, introductory
channel

[shorthand outlines]

, *when* clause
, conjunction

[shorthand outlines]

quality
familiar

intercommunication
instant
, when clause

directory
, series

independently
overloading
personnel

, if clause
demonstration

LESSON 62

459. BRIEF-FORM DERIVATIVES

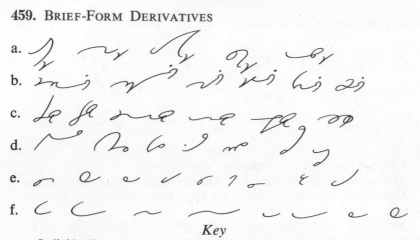

a.

b.

c.

d.

e.

f.

Key

a. Individualist, greatest, automobilist, accompanist, likeliest.

b. Schoolhouse, customhouse, courthouse, storehouse, poorhouse, warehouse.

c. Generalize, particularize, circularize, recognize, merchandise, characterize.

d. Delivery, difficulty, party, handy, worthy, every, referee.

e. Weak, where, were, what, with, wish, when, was, want.

f. Present, please, correct, glad, are, will, were, where.

460. GEOGRAPHICAL EXPRESSIONS

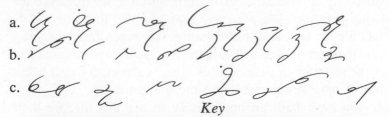

a.

b.

c.

Key

a. Pittsburgh, Harrisburg, Greensburg, Bloomsburg, Newburgh, Gettysburg.

b. South Dakota, Tennessee, Texas, Utah, Vermont, Virginia, West Virginia, Wisconsin.

c. Palestine, Singapore, Tokyo, Havana, San Diego, Rio de Janeiro.

CHAPTER XIII

461. Preview and Writing Practice

PREVIEW FOR LETTER 462.

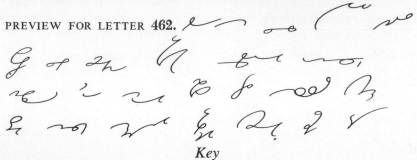

Key

Telegram, immediately, tomorrow, two or three.

Appreciate, initial, we are sure, obtainable, materials, workmanship.

Unexcelled, superior, qualities, we hope that, particularly, guarantee, defects.

Assistance, connection, consultants, specialists, developing, efficient, system.

462. Dear Mr. Black: Thank you very much for your telegram reading, "Send us immediately one four-drawer steel filing[1] cabinet No. 842."

Your telegram was received this morning, and the order is now in the hands[2] of our Shipping Department. The file will be sent out no later than tomorrow morning, and you should have it within[3] two or three days.

We sincerely appreciate receiving this initial order from you for one of our steel files. We are sure[4] that you will find this widely used steel file the best that is obtainable. It is made from the finest materials[5] that can be obtained, and the workmanship is unexcelled. Despite the superior qualities of this filing[6] cabinet, the cost is less' than that of most ordinary files on the market today.

After you have had[7] an opportunity to use this file, we hope that you will add more of them to your Filing Department. We are[8] particularly happy to call your attention to our one-year guarantee covering any defects in[9] materials or workmanship during the first year's use.

If you should have need of assistance in connection with[10] any of your filing problems, please feel free to call on us for the services of any of our consultants.[11] We shall be glad to send one of our specialists to your office at no cost to you. These consultants are well trained[12] in developing the most efficient filing system for every type of business. Yours very truly,[13] (260)

READING AND WRITING PRACTICE

463.

Transcribe:
No. 842

, parenthetical
specialists
exists

, *as* clause

, *if* clause
grateful

, introductory
inconvenient

up to date
no noun,
no hyphen

464.

experienced
, apposition

, nonrestrictive
, year date
analyzing
1936 ⊙
; because of comma
procedures

, *if* clause

465.

, *when* clause
happiness
clients

, *and* omitted
healthy
absent

, introductory

.

; illustrative ,
preference

pleasant
equipped
, parenthetical

, parenthetical

: enumeration
, series
salary

, introductory

, introductory
handsome

, *if* clause

466.

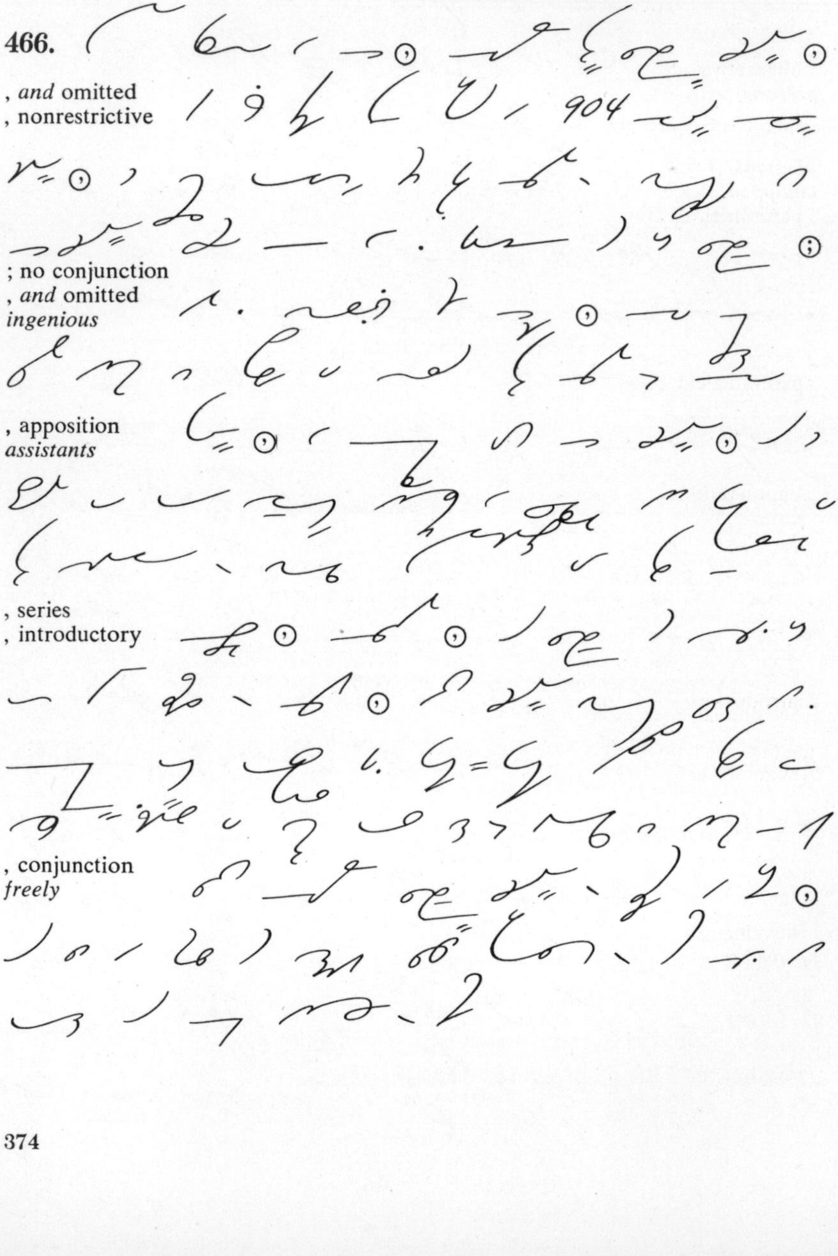

, *and* omitted
, nonrestrictive

; no conjunction
, *and* omitted
ingenious

, apposition
assistants

, series
, introductory

, conjunction
freely

LESSON 63

467. USEFUL BUSINESS-LETTER PHRASES

A OMITTED

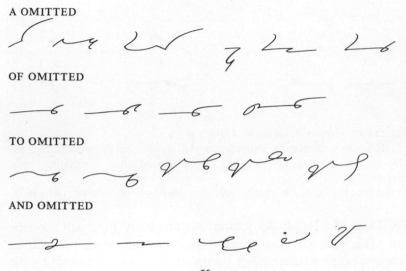

OF OMITTED

TO OMITTED

AND OMITTED

Key

At a time, at a loss, for a long time, in a position, for a moment, for a minute.

Many of the, many of those, many of them, how many of them.

Glad to see, glad to say, I should like to see, I should like to know, I should like to have.

Men and women, more and more, less and less, here and there, up and down.

468. FREQUENT NAMES

a.

b.

Key

a. O'Brien, O'Donnell, Olsen, Parker, Philips, Quinn, Roberts.
b. Laura, Lillian, Margaret, Marian, Martha.

469. PREVIEW AND WRITING PRACTICE

PREVIEW FOR LETTER **470.**

Key

Inventory, simplify, accurate, Cunningham.

Preliminaries, tabulating, extended, sorted, results, to us, process, listings.

Up to date, concentrate, thinking, routine, headaches, calculating, transcription.

Economical, local, to make, recommendations, of course, obligation.

470. Dear Mr. Reed: As you know, inventory time will soon be here. This year you can greatly simplify your work by[1] getting accurate, ready-to-use reports prepared from punched cards by the Cunningham Punched-Card Services.

Why bother[2] with time-consuming preliminaries when you can have your complete inventory data punched into[3] tabulating cards? When you use Cunningham's service, your inventory data can be extended at 1,000[4] extensions an hour, sorted at 15,000 cards an hour, and your inventory reports produced at 4,000[5] tickets an hour.

Here is how the service works: You take your inventory and send the results to us.[6] We process the results and send you complete listings. The reports you get are up to date, accurate, and well organized.[7] You can concentrate on the part of the job that takes thinking, and we will take care of the routine.

We take on[8] the headaches; that is, the sorting, calculating, and printing of reports in our office. You get accurate reports[9] because errors in transcription and posting are eliminated. The reports are economical, too,[10] because the same cards are used again and again after they are once punched.

All you need do to obtain this service[11] is to call your local Cunningham dealer; he will send an expert to your office to make recommendations.[12] The visit of this expert will, of course, place you under no financial obligation. Yours very truly,[13] (260)

READING AND WRITING PRACTICE

471.

, parenthetical
decisions

, *and* omitted
accurate

, parenthetical
, series

, series
analyze
execute

, apposition
: introducing
long quote

(shorthand outlines)

. inside quote

472.

, *if* clause
hourly

, series
overtime

double-barreled
hyphenated
before noun

10-key
hyphenated
before noun
, *and* omitted

, *if* clause
, parenthetical
obligation

; no conjunction
coupon

473.

audio-visual
preliminary

situations
possible

, when clause
undoubtedly

, introductory
principal
director

worth while
no noun,
no hyphen

, introducing
short quote
. inside quote

, parenthetical

474.

photocopy

, *and* omitted
color

utilization
, conjunction

LESSON 64

475. WORD BEGINNINGS

DIS-

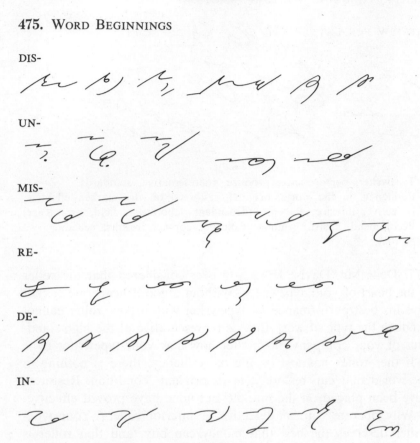

UN-

MIS-

RE-

DE-

IN-

Key

Dishonor, disinclined, disinterested, undisclosed, disadvantage, disuse.

Uninteresting, unenterprising, uninterrupted, unmindful, unmarried.

Misinterpret, misinterpreted, misconception, mistranslate, misfortune, mispronounce.

Re-examine, re-export, re-enact, re-enforce, re-elect.

Deceive, deceit, deceitful, decent, decently, decency, decentralize.

Incomplete, incompetent, inconsistent, inconvenience, incontestable, inconspicuous.

CHAPTER XIII

476. PREVIEW AND WRITING PRACTICE

PREVIEW FOR LETTER **477.**

Key

Typewriter, performance, produce, representative, standards.
Resiliency, in the world, original, restorers, on the market, effective.
Defective, inferior, Platen, independent, laboratory, field, experience.
Recommend, insist, genuine, Chicago, contact, results, schedule, we
hope that.

477. Dear Mr. Davis: Have you ever considered that the roller
is the heart of your typewriter? Without a good[1] heart one cannot
give his best performance. A typewriter with a poor roller cannot
produce the type of work that[2] is representative of the high standards of your company, no matter how new your typewriter is.

If the[3] roller has lost its life or resiliency, there is nothing in
the world that can restore it to its original[4] condition. Restorers
have been placed on the market, but none have proved effective.

Why operate with a[5] defective or inferior roller? Your typewriter deserves the best that money can buy, and that roller is
the[6] Ames All-Star Platen.

As the world's largest independent manufacturer of rollers and
repair parts, we feel[7] qualified, through laboratory tests, field
records, and fifty years' experience, to recommend the replacement[8] of rollers once a year. Insist on genuine Ames All-Star
Platens in the original wrapper.

Your friendly[9] Jackson Office Supply dealer in Chicago will
contact you within the next few days to tell you that he has[10]

Ames All-Star Platens in stock. He can save money for you and enable you to produce better results with a regular[11] schedule for changing your rollers at least every twelve months.

We hope that you will have Mr. Jackson[12] replace all your rollers that have been used for one year or more. Yours very truly, (254)

READING AND WRITING PRACTICE

478.

piece
precision
, parenthetical

, apposition
receiver

, when clause

loose
, series

compiled
percentage

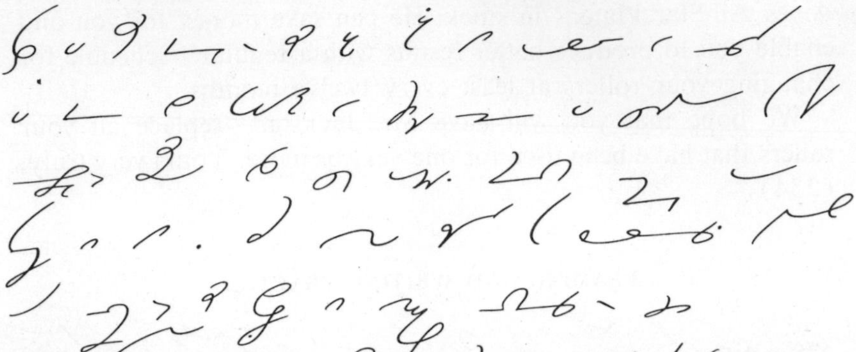

479.

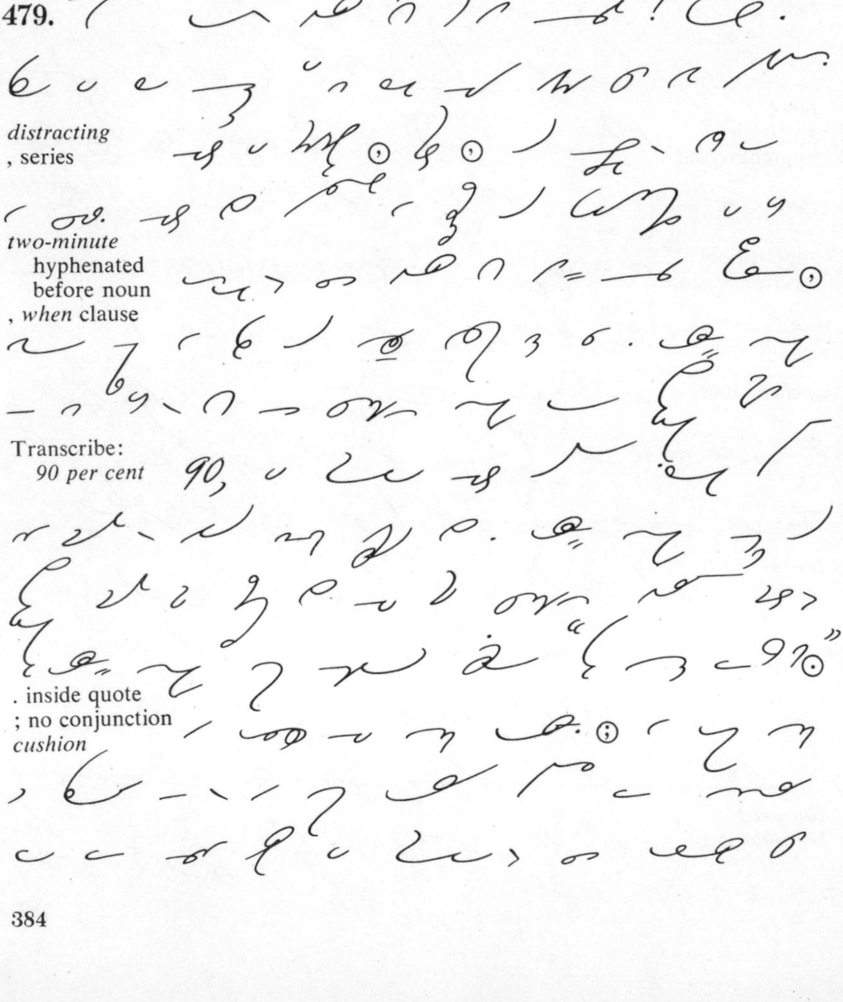

distracting
, series

two-minute
hyphenated before noun
, *when* clause

Transcribe:
90 per cent

. inside quote
; no conjunction
cushion

handsome
, and omitted
, when clause

. courteous
request

480.
, introducing
short quote
. inside quote

, series
secretary
treasurer

, year date
associating

peculiar
: enumeration

up to date
  no noun,
  no hyphen

prospectus
, series

; no conjunction
, introductory
material

, introductory
; no conjunction
, introductory

world's
privileges
; illustrative ,

LESSON 65

481. WORD-BUILDING PRACTICE — BLENDS

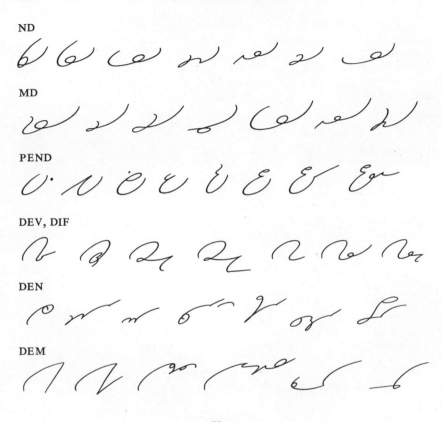

ND

MD

PEND

DEV, DIF

DEN

DEM

Key

Bind, brand, planned, second, trend, wind, land.

Framed, seemed, famed, named, blamed, trimmed, fumed.

Pending, depend, happened, opened, suspend, expend, expended, expenditure.

Devote, devise, develop, development, differ, different, difference.

Deny, student, wooden, identical, evident, accident, abandon.

Damage, damaged, domestic, demonstrate, seldom, medium.

READING AND WRITING PRACTICE

482. The Gift of Voice

cultural
separates
primitive

, parenthetical
characteristic

throughout
; illustrative ,

, series
agreeable

, series

familiar
adage
. inside quote

, *and* omitted
; no conjunction
develop

, *if* clause
, parenthetical

eloquent
monotonous

, *and* omitted
well-modulated
hyphenated
before noun

, parenthetical
, *and* omitted

, apposition
Demosthenes

CHAPTER XIII

pronunciation
, introductory

[shorthand]

, *and* omitted

[shorthand]

, conjunction
articulation

[shorthand]

; because of comma
, *if* clause
pronouncing

[shorthand]

; because of comma
, parenthetical

[shorthand]

theater
, parenthetical

[shorthand]

483. Developing Your Vocabulary

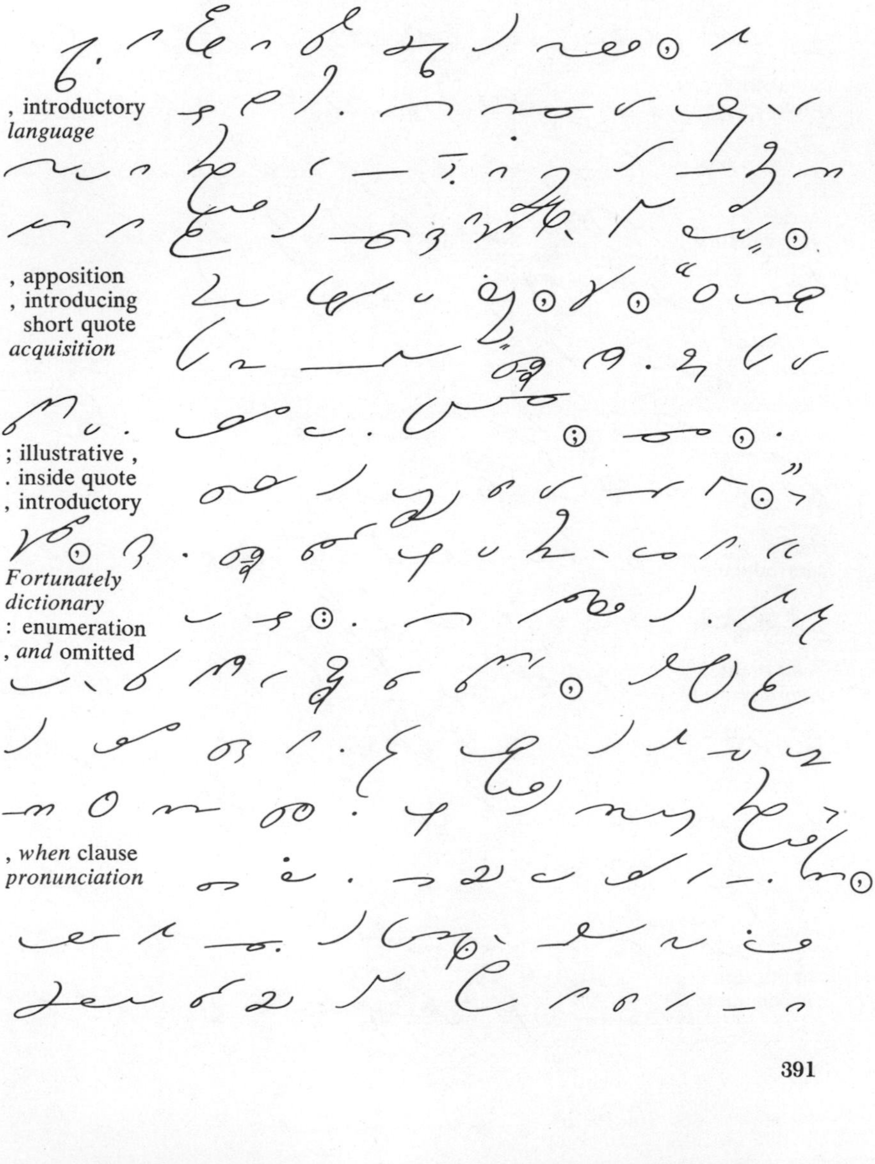

, introductory
language
, apposition
, introducing short quote
acquisition
; illustrative ,
. inside quote
, introductory
Fortunately
dictionary
: enumeration
, *and* omitted
, *when* clause
pronunciation

, introductory

; no conjunction

, apposition
conveys

, series
, introductory

choice
, introductory

, *and* omitted
vigorous

, apposition
. inside quote

CHAPTER XIV

LESSON 66

484. WORD FAMILIES

-TRACT

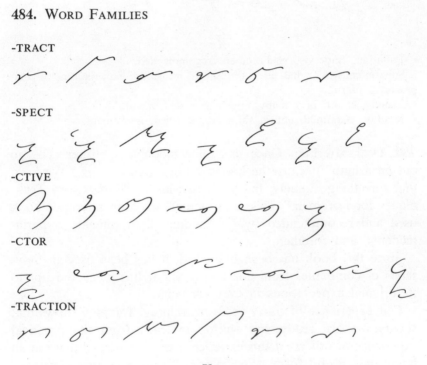

-SPECT

-CTIVE

-CTOR

-TRACTION

Key

Subtract, detract, retract, extract, attract, contract.
Respect, self-respect, disrespect, inspect, aspect, prospect, expect.
Defective, effective, attractive, collective, elective, respective.
Inspector, elector, conductor, collector, contractor, projector.
Subtraction, attraction, distraction, detraction, extraction, contraction.

485. Preview and Writing Practice

PREVIEW FOR LETTER **486.**

Key

Publisher, Supervisory, Foremen, recommended.

Superintendents, it has been, thousands, measured, expectations, respect, practical, useful.

Exactly, credit, how many, approval, tested, manual.

Readily, examined, entire, shipment, satisfied, investment.

486. Dear Mr. Lee: Once in a blue moon a publisher can "go out on a limb" because he knows he has a sure thing.[1] We have that sure thing; namely, the latest revision of "Supervisory Techniques for Foremen." This is an actual[2] working reference book used and recommended by outstanding plant officials, superintendents, and foremen.[3]

Since this book has been published, it has been used in thousands of companies from coast to coast. It has measured up[4] to its original expectations in every respect.

Our experience of thirty years of training[5] foremen shows that supervisors are ready and willing to learn from the practical experience of others[6] if this experience is presented to them in an interesting, useful form. "Supervisory Techniques[7] for Foremen" is exactly that type of publication.

The book sells for $6. We are willing to send a[8] copy on credit for each of your supervisors. Just let us know how many supervisors you have on your[9] staff; we will send you on approval enough copies of this tested manual for each of them. If your men feel[10] that they cannot readily use this manual after they have examined it, we shall be glad to have you return[1] the entire shipment. We will give you full credit. You pay for the books only when you are satisfied that you are[12] getting a return on your investment.

Are your supervisors worth $6 each to you? Sincerely yours,[13] (260)

READING AND WRITING PRACTICE

487.

, introductory
, introducing
short quote
. inside quote

, introductory
co-operation

worth while
no noun,
no hyphen

488.

. inside quote

[shorthand]

, when clause
ideally

[shorthand]

guide
reviewing

[shorthand]

, introductory
reactions

[shorthand]

, nonrestrictive
instructional

[shorthand]

, *if* clause

[shorthand]

489. *[shorthand]*

Employee
, apposition

[shorthand]

[shorthand outlines]

, introductory

. , nonrestrictive
inside quote
, year date

typical
, *if* clause

.

490.
response
, introductory
, apposition

, nonrestrictive
inside quote
, year date

, conjunction
appreciate
copies

491.
Mystery
; no conjunction
, introductory

CHAPTER XIV

[shorthand]

. inside quote

, introductory

detective
, introductory

: enumeration

best-written
hyphenated
before noun
, introductory

LESSON 67

492. Brief-Form Derivatives

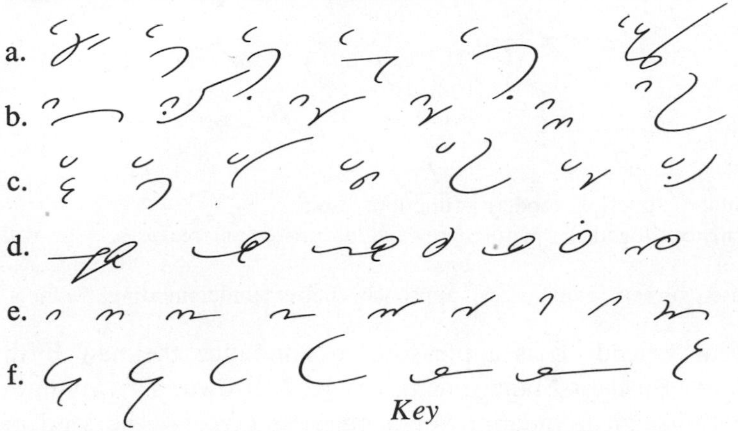

Key

a. Self-satisfied, self-confidence, self-covering, self-importance, self- governing, self-opinionated.

b. Undergo, underhanded, understand, understate, underworld, undervalue.

c. Overalls, overconfident, overtime, overuse, overvalue, overstate, overhand.

d. Merchandise, likewise, recognize, side, right, high, otherwise.

e. You, world, wonder, one, worth, yours truly, wish, to, success.

f. Purpose, probable, present, bill, remit, remember, speak, such.

493. Geographical Expressions

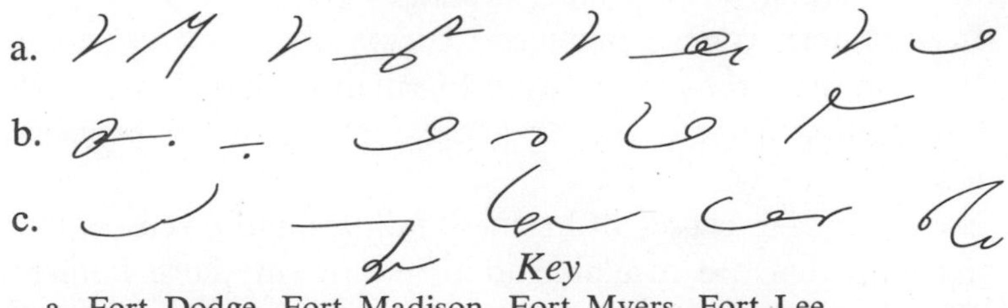

Key

a. Fort Dodge, Fort Madison, Fort Myers, Fort Lee.

b. Wyoming, New Hampshire, Louisiana, Kentucky, Florida, Delaware.

c. London, Manchester, Bristol, Plymouth, Edinburgh.

494. PREVIEW AND WRITING PRACTICE

PREVIEW FOR LETTER **495.**

Key

Announce, superior, modern, function, itself.

Administer, together, picture, reviewing, professor, features, you will find, short.

Concise, survey, emphasizes, approach, better understanding, failures.

495. Dear Friend: It is a pleasure to announce the new Fifth Edition of "Business Management," by R. J. Brown. This volume[1] gives a thorough foundation for a business career — the kind of superior training given in modern[2] colleges. It deals with the organization, function, and understanding of business itself. Students who are[3] training to administer business, work in business, or teach business must know how the parts of business work together.[4] Doctor Brown's book presents a full picture of business management. After reviewing this book, a well-known professor[5] stated, "It's the best book ever published in the field of management."

Here are a few of the many excellent[6] features you will find in the Fifth Edition of "Business Management":

1. It is a short, concise one-term[7] survey course.
2. It emphasizes the organization of small businesses and uses that approach for a[8] better understanding of big business, too.
3. It explains the causes of business failures and discusses the[9] agencies that are available to help prevent those failures.
4. "Business Management" is illustrated with photographs,[10] drawings, and charts to help stimulate interest and to assure perfect clarity.

5. At the end of each[11] chapter there are questions, projects, and recommended readings.

These are just a few of the features in this new[12] edition of "Business Management." Return the enclosed card, and we will send you an examination copy[13] immediately. Your very truly, (264)

READING AND WRITING PRACTICE

496.

Advertiser's
, apposition
inside quote

volume
, nonrestrictive

, introductory

glance
, when clause

five-day
  hyphenated
  before noun

, *if* clause
canceled

497.

, conjunction
referred

, introductory
campaign

*developing
principles*
, introductory

. inside quote
, introductory
, *as* clause

forcefully
, introductory

498.

, introductory

questionnaires
reactions

, year date
; because of comma
appreciative

1940

, introductory

evaluate
appeared

(shorthand outlines)

, conjunction
ranging

year's

499.

, if clause
already
evaluation

, nonrestrictive

, apposition
eastern

. courteous
request

LESSON 68

500. USEFUL BUSINESS-LETTER PHRASES

OR OMITTED

OF OMITTED

THE OMITTED

YOU OMITTED

Key

Day or two, one or two, two or three, three or four, more or less.

One of the, one of our, one of those, one of them, one of these, out of the, out of town.

By the way, in the future, in the world, about the matter, in the matter, in the market.

Will you please, will you please write, will you please send, will you please see.

501. FREQUENT NAMES

a.

b.

Key

a. Robertson, Robinson, Rogers, Russell, Ryan, Schmidt, Schneider, Scott.

b. Norman, Oliver, Owen, Patrick, Peter, Philip, Rudolph.

CHAPTER XIV

502. PREVIEW AND WRITING PRACTICE

PREVIEW FOR LETTER **503.**

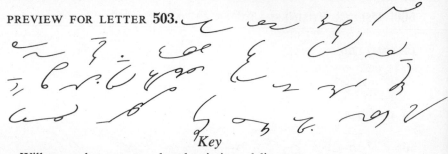

Key

Will you please, renewal, subscription, delivery.

Electrical, interruption, a hundred, slightest, possibility, prompt, current.

Interested, I believe, continuing, beyond, optimistic, reason, constant, interviews.

Prominent, undoubtedly, beneficial, anxious, reporting, grateful, up-to-date.

503. Dear Subscriber: May we ask a favor?

Will you please initial and return the enclosed Renewal Form even[1] though your subscription still has several weeks to run.

This will insure the delivery of your copies of The[2] Modern Electrical Age without interruption. Actually, there is just one chance in a hundred that you[3] might miss an issue at renewal time; but if you renew now, you will remove even the slightest possibility[4] of error. Your prompt reply will enable us to enter your renewal well in advance of the current[5] expiration date of your subscription.

As one of those good friends of ours, you will be interested, I believe,[6] in learning that our magazine is continuing to grow beyond what was expected by the most optimistic[7] of us a year or so ago.

There is a very good reason for this; namely, the constant effort by[8] our news staff to improve the magazine. The series of interviews with prominent men has undoubtedly attracted[9] wide attention; and we know, from letters received from our readers, that these interviews are most beneficial[10] to them.

Our editors are more anxious than ever to learn about you and what kind of news and news reporting[11] best fits your needs. That explains the information card also enclosed.

We shall be grateful for any suggestions[12] you can give us. They all help to make The Modern Electrical Age a better, more up-to-date publication.[13] Sincerely yours, (262)

READING AND WRITING PRACTICE

504.

, nonrestrictive
subscription

, parenthetical

envelope
; no conjunction

family
, introductory

505.

16-month
hyphenated
before noun

, introductory
particularly

worth while
no noun,
no hyphen
, conjunction

16

506.

, *if* clause
thousands

, introductory

percentage

, introductory
Digest

activities

, conjunction
subscribers

507.

, *as* clause
, introducing
  short quote
"

. inside quote
, introductory

; because of comma

409

, apposition
, *when* clause
apparent

, introductory
immediately

508.

permission
, *if* clause

single-copy
   hyphenated
   before noun
, nonrestrictive

, introductory

LESSON 69

509. WORD ENDINGS

-ULT

-ULATOR

-ICALLY

-MENTARY

-INGS

-INGLY

Key

Consult, consults, consulted, consultation, result, results, resulted, resultant.

Regulator, speculator, insulator, tabulator, calculator, circulator.

Periodically, technically, mechanically, practically, critically.

Elementary, complementary, supplementary, momentary.

Dealings, preachings, buildings, earnings, clippings, beginnings.

Unwillingly, disparagingly, uncompromisingly, unfeelingly, unknowingly, unthinkingly.

411

510. PREVIEW AND WRITING PRACTICE

PREVIEW FOR LETTER **511.**

PREVIEW FOR LETTER **512.**

Key

Article, conditions, last month's, enjoyed.

Definitely, contribute, toward, better understanding, typical, certainly, one year's.

To know, interest, you will be able, comments.

Bulletin, areas, indicate, clippings, 10 cents, minimum, effort.

511. Dear Mr. Allen: Thank you for sending me the article on present credit conditions, which was taken from[1] last month's issue of Credit News. I have enjoyed reading this article, and I definitely feel that it has much[2] to contribute toward a better understanding of present credit conditions in our country.

If this article[3] is typical of those that appear each month in your magazine, I certainly want to be one of your subscribers.[4] Enclosed are the completed subscription form and my check for $5 for a one year's subscription. Yours truly,[5]

512. Dear Mr. White: Here is an opportunity to know what the newspapers are saying that is of interest[6] to you. Through the use of our press clipping service, you will be able at a small cost to keep in touch with the press[7] comments that will help you in your business.

Our service covers all the major newspapers in the country. As you[8] will see by the enclosed bulletin, our service is divided into several areas. Merely indicate[9] the area of your major interest, and you will receive clippings from newspapers serving that section[10] of the country.

The cost of the service is 10 cents a clipping, with a minimum charge of $10 a month.[11] When you consider the vast amount of time and the effort that are required to go through just one newspaper[12] for items of interest, you realize what a great saving our service can be to you. Yours very truly,[13] (260)

READING AND WRITING PRACTICE

513.

widely read
no hyphen
after ly

well known
no noun,
no hyphen
; illustrative ,

cartoon
, parenthetical

, apposition
American

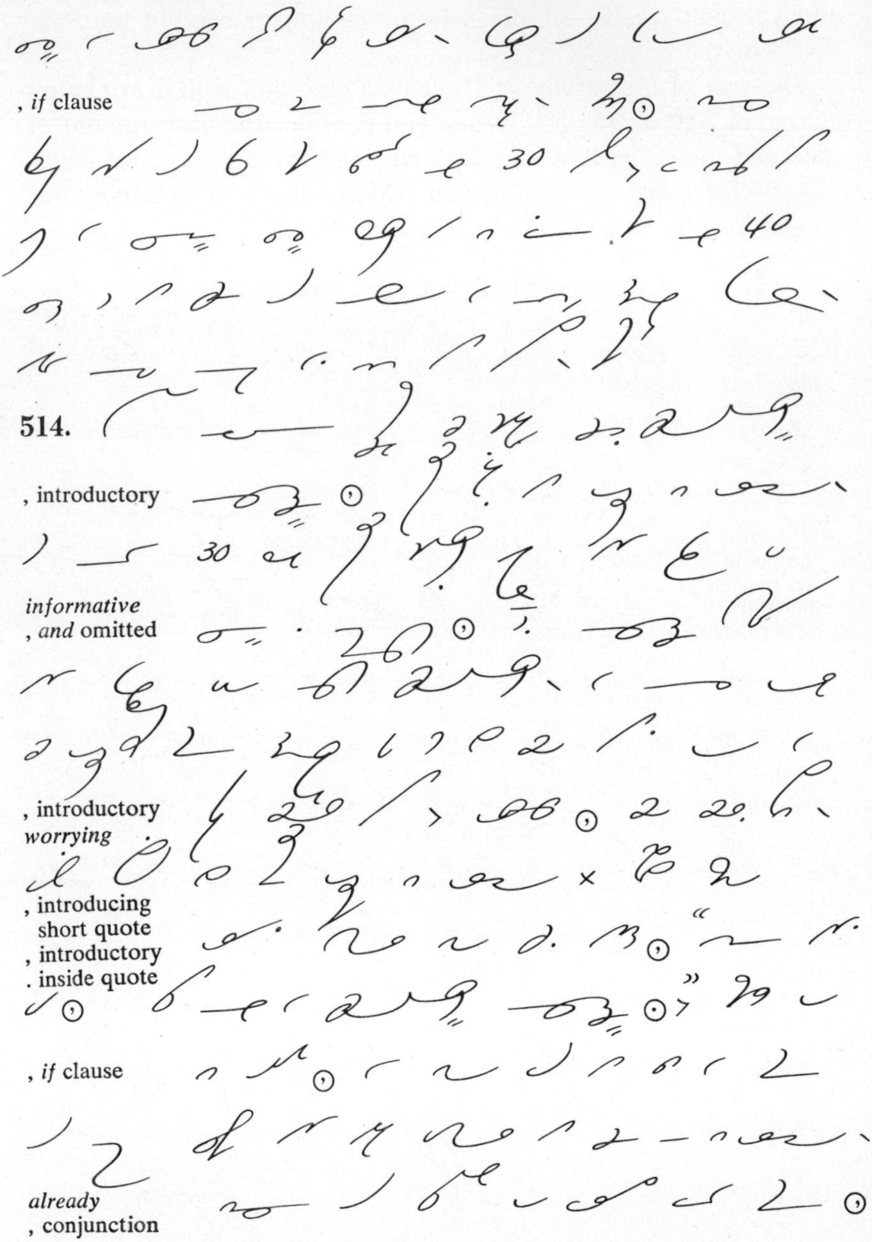

, *if* clause

514.

, introductory

informative
, *and* omitted

, introductory
worrying

, introducing short quote
, introductory
. inside quote

, *if* clause

already
, conjunction

515.

appeared
month's

survey
businessmen

gratifying
continuation

, apposition
thousands
abreast

up-to-date
 hyphenated
  before noun

, when clause

516.

, parenthetical
secretary's

, series
syllabication

385

; no conjunction
invaluable

LESSON 70

517. WORD-BUILDING PRACTICE — EXPRESSION OF *w*

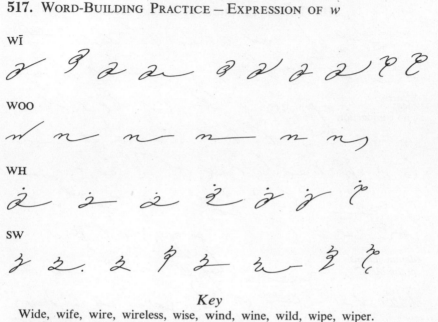

Key
Wide, wife, wire, wireless, wise, wind, wine, wild, wipe, wiper.
Wood, wool, woolen, woman, wonder, wolf.
While, whim, whale, whistle, white, whiten, whip.
Sweet, swelling, swing, switch, swim, swollen, swift, sweepings.

518. ACCURACY PRACTICE — DIPHTHONGS

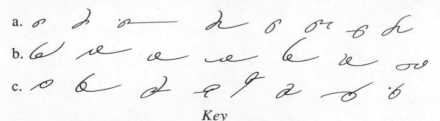

Key
a. Use, few, human, fuel, out, ounce, now, power.
b. Point, toil, oil, royal, boil, soil, annoy.
c. Tie, pile, fine, nice, dine, wire, guide, height.

CHAPTER XIV

READING AND WRITING PRACTICE

519. The Declaration of Independence

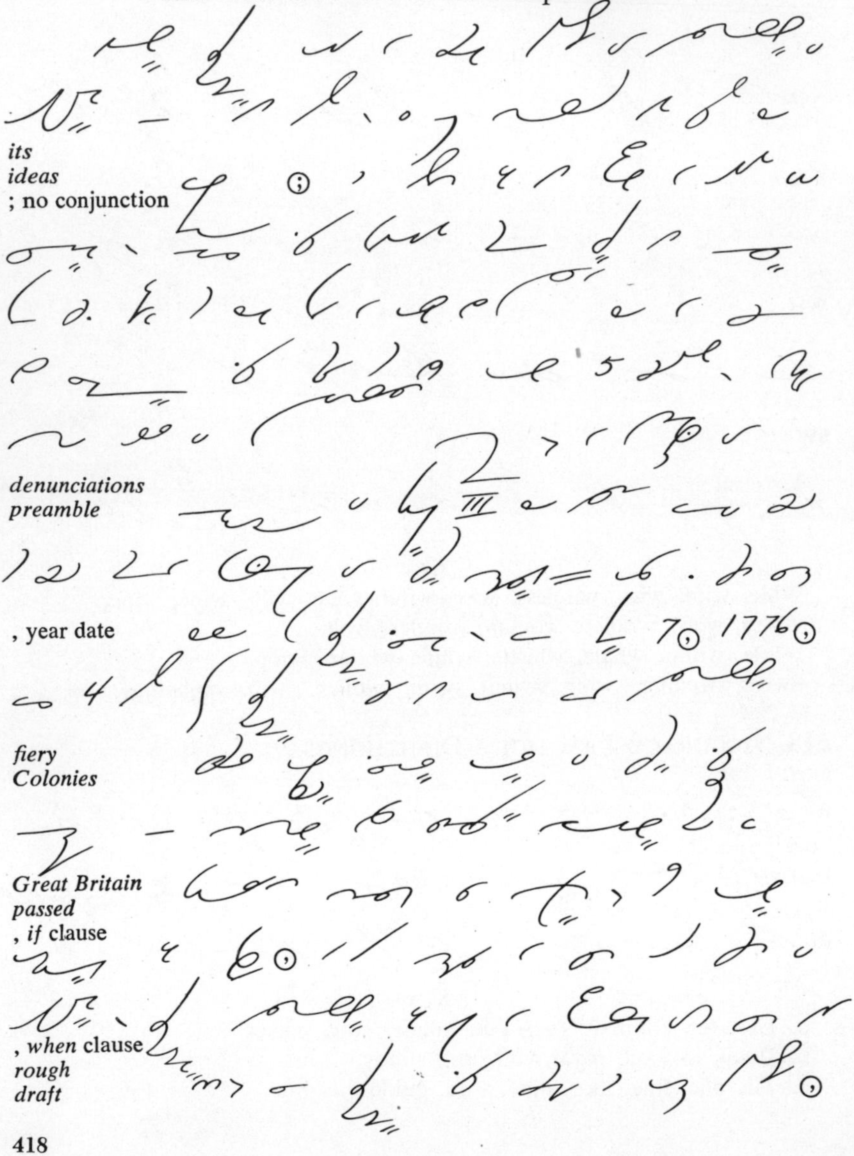

its
ideas
; no conjunction

denunciations
preamble

, year date

fiery
Colonies

Great Britain
passed
, *if* clause

, *when* clause
rough
draft

, apposition

, year date
; because of comma

, apposition
, *as* clause

, *when* clause

hearts
fateful

, parenthetical
; because of comma

; illustrative ,

. inside quote
, parenthetical

assemblies
, series

Hancock
affixed
, apposition

, conjunction
degrees

; no conjunction
losing

[Shorthand outlines with margin annotations:]

; because of comma
, parenthetical

, parenthetical
galloped

, introductory
; because of comma

, parenthetical

Matlack
, conjunction

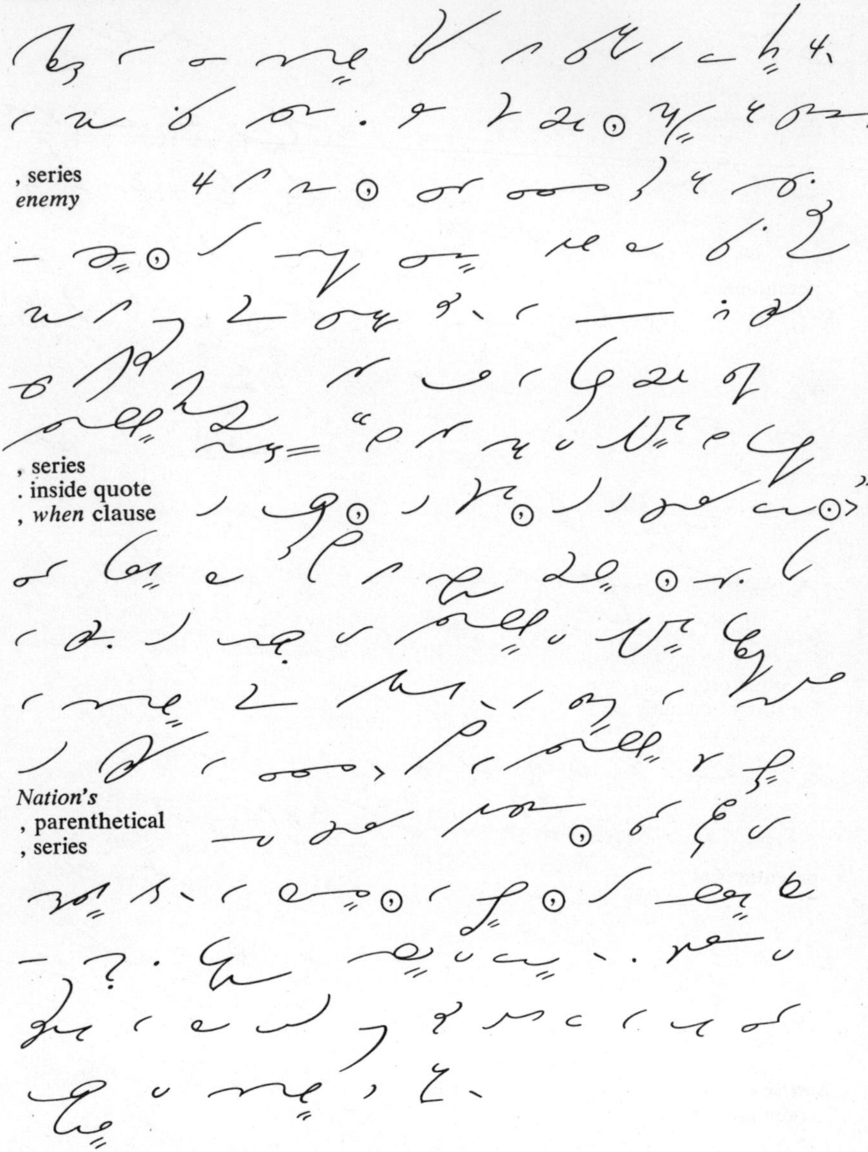

, series
enemy

, series
. inside quote
, *when* clause

Nation's
, parenthetical
, series

LESSON 71

520. WORD FAMILIES

UNN-

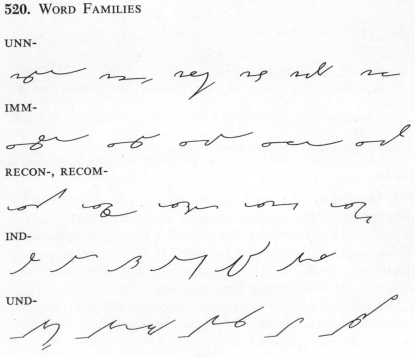

IMM-

RECON-, RECOM-

IND-

UND-

Key

Unnatural, unnumbered, unnerved, unnecessary, unnoticed, unknown.
Immaterial, immature, immortal, immoral, immodest.
Recondition, reconcile, reconstruct, recommission, recompense.
Index, indirect, induce, indulge, independent, indiscreet.
Undiscovered, undisclosed, undismayed, undue, undoubtedly.

CHAPTER XV

521. PREVIEW AND WRITING PRACTICE

PREVIEW FOR LETTER **522.**

PREVIEW FOR LETTER **523.**

Key

Application, membership, Atlantic.

Organization, composed, improving, industry, maintained, objective, certain.

Essential, financial, appreciate, of course, furnish, confidential, eligibility, as soon as.

Requested, connection, adequate, various.

To us, activities, heard, articles, monthly, will you please, as soon as possible.

522. Gentlemen: We are happy to receive your application for membership in the Atlantic Luggage Association.[1] This organization, which is composed of the leading luggage manufacturers in the West, was organized[2] in June, 1938, for the purpose of improving conditions in the industry. It has maintained[3] that objective ever since it was first organized.

We are enclosing an information report form that[4] will give our membership committee certain essential facts about the history, organization, and financial standing[5] of your company. We shall greatly appreciate your completing this form and returning it immediately.[6] It is, of course, understood that all information that you furnish is entirely confidential and[7] will be used by our organization solely to determine your eligibility for membership.

As[8] soon as we receive the report, your application will be submitted to our membership committee. Yours truly,[9]

523. Dear Mr. Smith: Enclosed is our completed information report that you requested in connection with our[10] application for membership in the Atlantic Luggage Association. We hope that the information[11] supplied is adequate for the purposes of your membership committee.

The various services provided[12] by your organization will be of great help to us in our business activities. Also, we have heard many[13] fine reports regarding the excellent articles appearing in Atlantic Luggage News, the monthly magazine[14] issued by the Association.

Will you please let us know as soon as possible whether our application[15] is accepted. Yours truly, (304)

READING AND WRITING PRACTICE

524.

manuscript
submitted

, conjunction
editorial
considerable

; no conjunction
, introductory
until

, if clause

525.

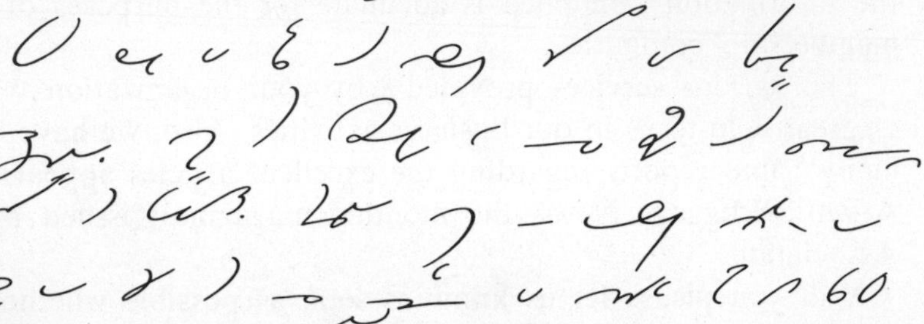

standard
, conjunction

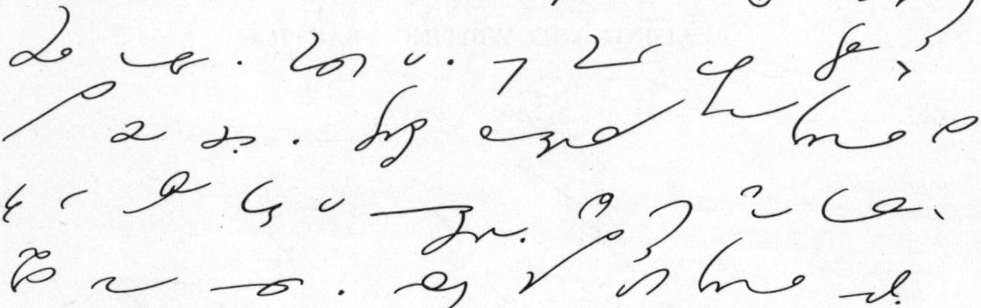

: enumeration
, *and* omitted
easy-to-understand
hyphenated
before noun

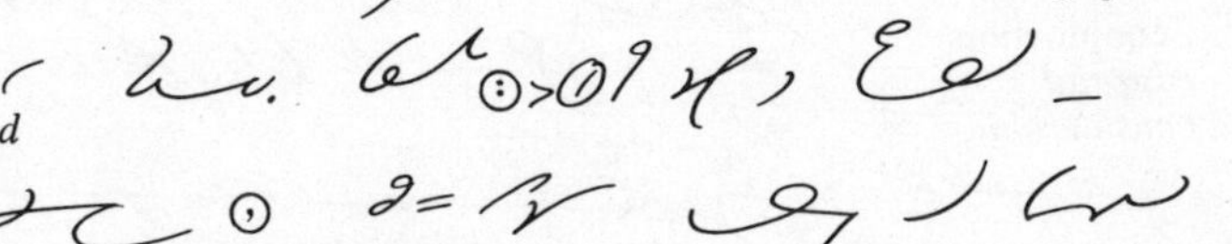

, series
, apposition

526.

: introducing
  long quote

, introductory
. inside quote

accessories
, introductory

527.

, conjunction
  inside quote
rural

CHAPTER XV

; illustrative ,
, series
on-the-job
  hyphenated
  before noun

overcrowded
, and omitted

, *if* clause
specific

428

LESSON 72

528. BRIEF-FORM DERIVATIVES

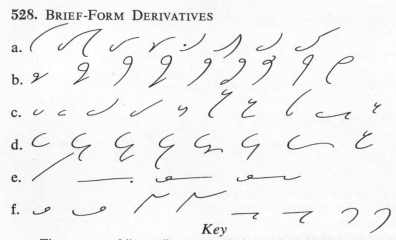

a.

b.

c.

d.

e.

f.

Key

a. Time, automobile, ordinary, stand, hand, individual, want, wanted.

b. Yesterday, after, advantage, advertise, ever, every, several, agent, about.

c. Of, all, want, order, office, object, opinion, body, always, was.

d. Present, purpose, property, probable, prosecute, purchase, progress, opportunity.

e. Date, morning, remember, remainder.

f. Regard, letter, doctor, deliver, must, important, confidence, cover.

529. GEOGRAPHICAL EXPRESSIONS

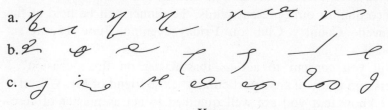

a.

b.

c.

Key

a. St. Charles, St. John, St. Paul, St. Lawrence, St. Louis.

b. Wisconsin, Rhode Island, California, Nebraska, Nevada, Maryland, Massachusetts.

c. Russia, Hungary, Tunis, Iran, Iraq, Africa, Asia.

CHAPTER XV

530. PREVIEW AND WRITING PRACTICE

PREVIEW FOR LETTER **531.**

[shorthand]

PREVIEW FOR LETTER **532.**

[shorthand]

Key

Few days ago, president, European, Los Angeles.
Organization, informal, already, acceptances, according, Oceanside, Club.
Toastmaster, I understand, qualified, ceremonies, program, appropriate.
Forward, Manufacturing, headquarters, beautiful.
Spacious, in the past, registration, indications, attendance, especially, outstanding, discussion.

531. Dear Mr. Lane: A few days ago I learned that our president, Mr. Carl Wilson, is planning to leave next month[1] for a European tour. He will not return to Los Angeles until early in the fall.

Several of[2] the men in our organization have decided to arrange an informal dinner for Mr. Wilson before[3] he leaves. I have already received acceptances from fifteen men in this company.

According to our[4] present plans, the dinner will be held at the Oceanside Country Club on Friday evening, June 15, at six o'clock.[5]

Will you consent to act as toastmaster on this occasion? I understand that you are a particularly[6] close friend of Mr. Wilson's, and I know that you are well qualified to act as master of ceremonies. Of[7] course, we shall not want to have a big program of speeches. I believe, however, that it would be appropriate[8] to call on a few of Mr. Wilson's friends.

Will you be able to serve as our toastmaster. Yours truly,[9]

532. Dear Mr. Trees: We should like to take this opportunity to tell you that we are looking forward to seeing you[10] at the National Manufacturing Convention in St. Louis, November 10 and 11. Headquarters[11] for our meeting this year will be in the beautiful, spacious Hunter Hotel.

In the past, our registration has[12] been approximately five hundred. This year all indications point to a greater attendance than ever before.[13]

The enclosed leaflet outlines the program for the two-day convention. This year's arrangement committee feels that[14] it has obtained an especially outstanding group of speakers and discussion leaders.

Will you be there? Yours truly,[15] (300)

<h3 style="text-align:center">READING AND WRITING PRACTICE</h3>

533.

reputation
community
, series

reasonable
, *as* clause

, nonrestrictive
, introductory

534.

(shorthand outlines)

; no conjunction
, introductory

, introductory
, *if* clause
manuals

well trained
no noun,
no hyphen

factors
, *when* clause
, conjunction

535.

contributors

, year date
: enumeration

; illustrative ,
children
weeks'

, introductory
distributed

various
; no conjunction

, introducing
short quote
. inside quote

536.

CHAPTER XV

Transcribe:
No. 2543
, parenthetical

, apposition
territory
St. Louis

, *if* clause

537.

, apposition

, *as* clause
specifications
accept

434

LESSON 73

538. USEFUL BUSINESS-LETTER PHRASES

OF OMITTED

TO OMITTED

IN OMITTED

THE OMITTED

Key

Some of the, some of them, some of those, some of our, some of these, some of this.

In addition to the, in addition to that, in addition to these, in addition to them, up to date, up to the minute, we should like to have.

Mother-in-law, father-in-law, brother-in-law, sister-in-law, son-in-law.

On the part, on the question, on the subject, upon the subject, on the whole.

539. FREQUENT NAMES

a.

b.

Key

a. Shaw, Shea, Simpson, Snyder, Stevens, Stewart, Sullivan, Taylor.
b. Pauline, Phyllis, Rachel, Rebecca, Ruth, Sarah, Sylvia.

435

CHAPTER XV

540. PREVIEW AND WRITING PRACTICE

PREVIEW FOR LETTER **541.**

PREVIEW FOR LETTER **542.**

Key

It has been, profitable, accountants, during the past month.

Appreciation, carefully, extensive, program, proposed, we are sure, substantial.

Competent, impartial, effect, recommendations, in regard, impersonal, interested.

Already, announcement, annual, Manufacturing.

Offices; Denver, Colorado; election, Directors, in addition, transacted, summary.

541. Dear Mr. Moore: It has been a pleasant and profitable experience to work with your cost accountants during[1] the past month. I wish to take this opportunity to express to you the appreciation of this company[2] for the results obtained thus far.

After carefully analyzing our department costs, your staff outlined[3] an extensive program for the more efficient operation of our factory. When all the proposed changes[4] have been made, we are sure that we shall realize a substantial decrease in operating expenses.

We are[5] now in agreement with you that a competent and impartial outside organization can often effect[6] improvements much more rapidly and easily than can members of one's own company. Because the recommendations[7] of your men in regard to changes were impersonal, we have been able to maintain the good will of[8] our staff.

It will be a pleasure to recommend your organization to anyone interested. Yours truly,[9]

542. Dear Friend: You perhaps have already seen an announcement in your local paper that reads: "Notice is hereby given[10] that the annual meeting of stockholders of the Lincoln Manufacturing Company will be held at its[11] offices in Denver, Colorado, on March 10, at 2 p.m. All voting members are urged to attend."

The[12] main order of business will be the election of a Board of Directors for the coming year. In addition, such[13] other business that may properly come before the meeting will be transacted.

Prior to the meeting, you will receive[14] a summary of the past year's operations, along with an outline of the plans for next year. Yours truly,[15] (300)

READING AND WRITING PRACTICE

543.

accordance
Maintenance
, introductory

, apposition
; because of comma
, parenthetical
despite

. courteous
request

[shorthand outline]

, conjunction
directory

[shorthand outline]

544.

[shorthand outline]

, *as* clause
, year date

[shorthand outline]

1945
Transcribe:
  $18,000
principal

[shorthand outline]

12/
, introductory
believe

[shorthand outline]

five-year
  hyphenated
  before noun
, introductory

[shorthand outline]

545.

[shorthand outline]

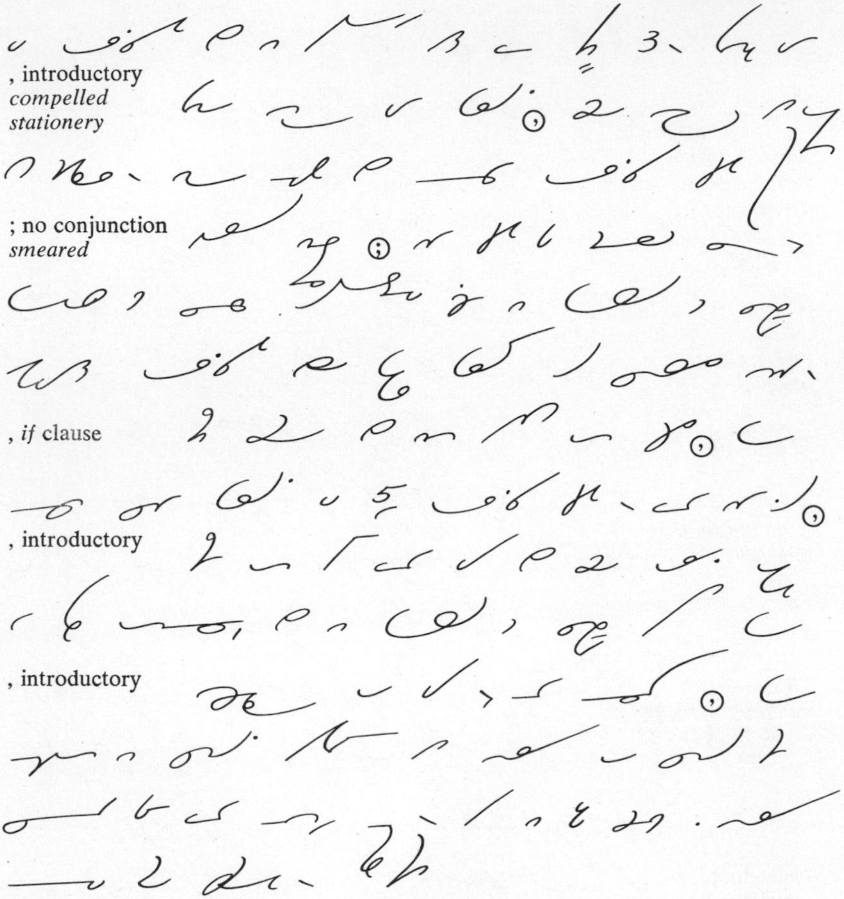

, introductory
compelled
stationery

; no conjunction
smeared

, *if* clause

, introductory

, introductory

546.

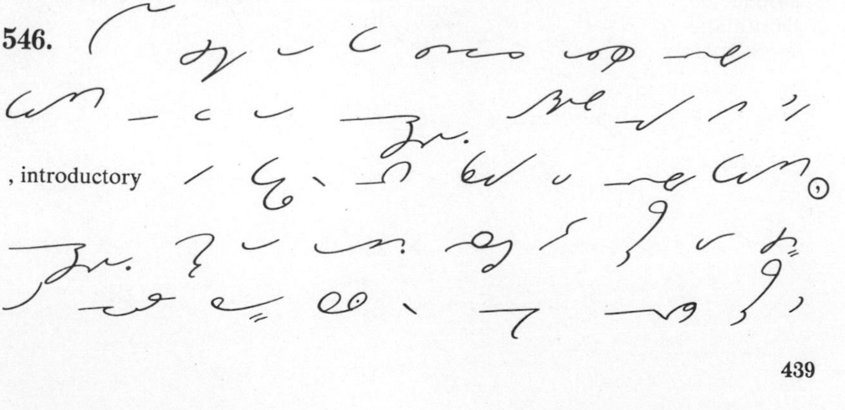

, introductory

, introductory
sites
access

, series
, *when* clause
unequaled

, *and* omitted
analysis

, *if* clause
carefully screened
no hyphen
after *ly*

, introductory
, introducing
short quote
. inside quote

547.

LESSON 74

548. WORD BEGINNINGS

SUB-

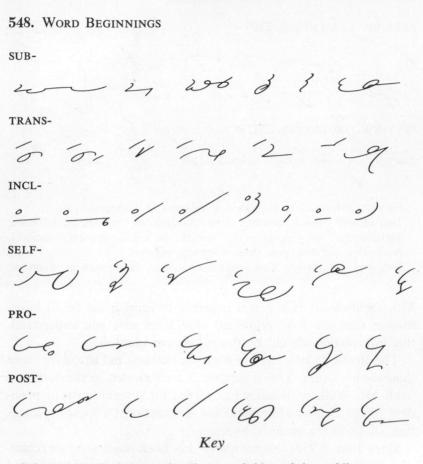

TRANS-

INCL-

SELF-

PRO-

POST-

Key

Subnormal, submission, subordinate, subside, subsist, sublime.

Transact, transacted, transient, transgression, transform, untranslatable.

Inclement, inclemency, include, included, inclusive, inclusion, incline, inclined.

Self-indulgent, self-sufficient, self-esteem, self-complacent, self-denial, self-possessed.

Promisingly, promulgate, proportion, proprietor, provide, project.

Postgraduate, posterity, postdate, postoperative, postscript, postponement.

CHAPTER XV

549. PREVIEW AND WRITING PRACTICE

PREVIEW FOR LETTER **550.**

[shorthand outlines]

PREVIEW FOR LETTER **551.**

[shorthand outlines]

Key

Furnish, information, requested, I am sure, confidential.

Detroit, well known, furniture, terms, Association, organization, has been.

Merchandise, invoices, promptly, custom, period, co-operate, whenever.

According, surveys, past year, America, survives.

Frequent, insufficient, Commercial, economic, circumstances, financial, won't.

550. Gentlemen: It is a real pleasure to furnish the credit information that you have requested. As[1] I am sure you understand, this information should be treated as confidential.

The Bradley Company has been[2] in business in Detroit for more than twenty years. This company is well known in the furniture field. Mr. William[3] Bradley has served for several terms as president of the Detroit Manufacturers Association,[4] a local organization of furniture manufacturers.

Since June, 1953, this company[5] has been purchasing merchandise from us on open account. All invoices have been paid promptly; in fact, it is[6] the custom of the company to pay our invoices within the discount period.

We are glad to co-operate[7] with you by furnishing this credit report. Whenever we can be of service to you again, please call[8] on us, as the sole purpose of our entire organization is to serve our members. Very truly yours,[9]

551. Dear Mr. Arthur: According to several national surveys conducted this past year, the average[10] manufacturing company in America survives less than ten years. The most frequent cause of failure is insufficient[11] capital.

The Commercial and Savings Bank, 1200 East Broadway, was organized in June, 1920,[12] to help manufacturing companies through difficult economic circumstances when capital[13] is scarce.

Our bank does not want you to risk losing your credit and your business in periods of financial stress.[14] Won't you come in soon and discuss with us any financial problems your company may have. Sincerely yours,[15] (300)

READING AND WRITING PRACTICE

552.

suffering
expense
, series

factories
, as clause

553.

well-planned
hyphenated
before noun

, parenthetical
nominal

; illustrative ,

554.

, conjunction
assistance

, nonrestrictive
idea

[shorthand outlines]

, parenthetical
; because of comma
minor

well-written
hyphenated
before noun
, *and* omitted
, nonrestrictive

555.

, introductory
, apposition
disagreement

[shorthand outlines]

, parenthetical

[shorthand outlines]

present-day
  hyphenated
  before noun

[shorthand outlines]

, introductory
union
employees

[shorthand outlines]

. courteous
  request

[shorthand outlines]

556.

drawing
typify

[shorthand outlines]

model
, parenthetical

[shorthand outlines]

, *when* clause
company's

[shorthand outlines]

LESSON 75

557. WORD-BUILDING — OMISSION OF *t* AND *d*

-CT

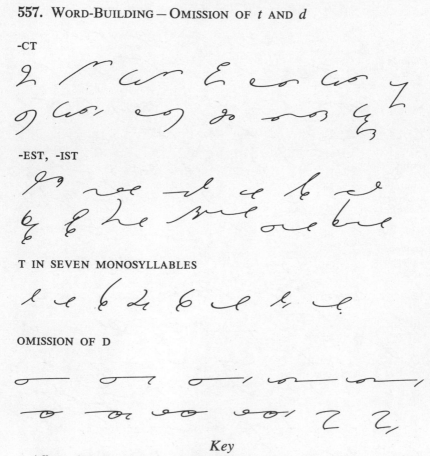

-EST, -IST

T IN SEVEN MONOSYLLABLES

OMISSION OF D

Key

Affect, deduct, product, expect, elect, protect, reject, active, protected, elective, exactly, neglects, prospects.

Darkest, cleanest, modest, honest, deepest, coldest, sharpest, typist, vocalist, industrialist, analyst, journalist.

Test, rest, best, first, past, last, tested, lasting.

Amend, amends, amended, recommend, recommended, mind, minds, remind, reminded, compound, compounded.

READING AND WRITING PRACTICE

558. History Of The Capitol Building

Nation's
eagle

, introductory
conception
Constitution

cannons
, year date

architect
Hallet
, apposition

Thornton

[Shorthand outlines]

dismissed
substituting

[Shorthand outlines]

, parenthetical
unforeseen

[Shorthand outlines]

crumbled
chandelier

[Shorthand outlines]

, parenthetical
befitted
era

[Shorthand outlines] 1812

[Shorthand outlines]

Great Britain
Potomac
, parenthetical

[Shorthand outlines] 1814

[Shorthand outlines]

, *when* clause
intact

Latrobe
, nonrestrictive

motifs
leaves

previous
carried

Bullfinch
, apposition
, parenthetical

13

1851

, series

bursting
seams
, conjunction

, nonrestrictive

; because of comma
, parenthetical

15

dilemma
; because of comma

, introductory
tier

, parenthetical
plaza
miracle

285,

, introductory
superbly
today's

, conjunction

, series
corridors

, introductory
galleries

splendors
, introductory

, series
carpenter's

LESSON 76

559. WORD FAMILIES

-HAND

-END

-FORMED

-TIVE

-SIGNED

Key

Hand, longhand, shorthand, backhand, beforehand, secondhand, fore-hand.

End, weakened, darkened, quickened, thickened, blackened.

Formed, reformed, informed, conformed, performed, deformed, un-informed.

Native, superlative, relative, informative, imaginative.

Signed, assigned, resigned, designed, countersigned, unsigned, redesigned.

CHAPTER XVI

560. PREVIEW AND WRITING PRACTICE

PREVIEW FOR LETTER **561.**

PREVIEW FOR LETTER **562.**

Key

Senior, secretarial, telephone, technique.

Have been, client, typical, discussions, future, to be sure, they would like to have, profit.

In regard, habits, describing, material.

We shall be glad, completed, unusual, interest, if you would like, to provide, furnish.

Operator, projector, facilities, readily, hesitate, if you desire, further.

561. Gentlemen: The senior secretarial students studying proper telephone technique at the Springfield School[1] of Business have been asking, "Is it correct to request a client to hold the line while you search for information?"[2] This question is typical of the many problems that have been brought up in our class discussions this past week.[3]

As future secretaries, these students want to be sure that they know proper telephone techniques; therefore they would[4] like to have some films, booklets, and records on using the telephone.

Would you please send us any information[5] you have on this subject. I am sure we shall all profit by reading and seeing this material. Yours truly,[6]

562. Dear Miss Lee: We are sorry we were unable to reach you by telephone in regard to your request for[7] information on correct telephone habits.

For your information, we are enclosing one copy each of several[8] booklets describing good telephone habits. If this is the type of material you had in mind for use in[9] your class, we shall be glad to send you as many copies as you request.

In June, 1953, our Company completed[10] two films that should be of unusual interest to your class. The titles of these two films are: "Proper Telephone[11] Techniques" and "Telephone Courtesy." If you would like to show either of these films, or both, to your class, we[12] shall be glad to provide them for you. We can also furnish the operator, the projector, and the screen if[13] these facilities are not readily available at your school.

Please do not hesitate to call our school representative,[14] Mr. R. A. Johnson, if you desire any further information. Yours very truly,[15] (300)

READING AND WRITING PRACTICE

563.

warehouse
, parenthetical

previous
, *as* clause

facilities
, conjunction

, parenthetical

...

CHAPTER XVI

distributing
, parenthetical
, nonrestrictive

computation
transcription
, series

, *if* clause
accept

hours'
, conjunction

564.

received

, series
calculating

456

well-equipped
hyphenated
before noun
, introductory

, introductory
Transcribe:
  2 p.m.

565.

; because of comma
, apposition
busy

, introductory

, *if* clause

CHAPTER XVI

, introductory
; no conjunction

[shorthand notation]

, conjunction

[shorthand notation]

566.

worth while
  no noun,
   no hyphen
. inside quote

[shorthand notation]

, *and* omitted
co-operative

[shorthand notation]

, apposition
colleagues

[shorthand notation]

LESSON 77

567. BRIEF-FORM DERIVATIVES

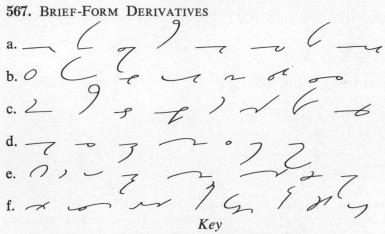

a.

b.

c.

d.

e.

f.

Key

a. Among, been, enable, ever, must, most, but, Mrs.
b. I, bill, next, else, one, etc., immediate.
c. From, advantage, necessary, merchant, for, could, between, matter.
d. Important, any, enough, gone, he, never, nevertheless.
e. This, is, our, newspaper, gone, got, send, unable.
f. Quantity, regular, throughout, suggest, prosecute, such, situation, refer.

568. GEOGRAPHICAL EXPRESSIONS

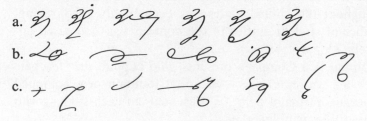

a.

b.

c.

Key

a. Westfield, West Haven, West Orange, Westview, West Bend, Westchester.
b. Philippine Islands, Guam, Alaska, Hawaii, Puerto Rico, Cuba.
c. Nova Scotia, Quebec, Ontario, Manitoba, Saskatchewan, British Columbia.

CHAPTER XVI

569. SMALL_CAPS PREVIEW AND WRITING PRACTICE

PREVIEW FOR LETTER **570.**

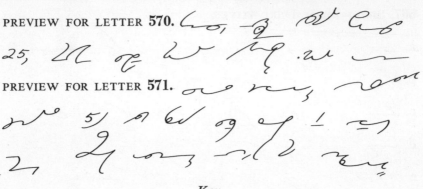

PREVIEW FOR LETTER **571.**

Key

Penmanship, enthusiasm, thousands, approximately.
25 per cent, fountain pen, equipped, folder, describes, awards, welcome.
Annually, scholarships, graduates.
Secondary, $500, tuition, period, equivalent, eligible, 100, qualify.
Information, available, recommendations, enclosed, further, Counselors.

570. Dear Mr. Gray: From September to February of this school year, the Capital Pen Company will again sponsor[1] its national shorthand penmanship contest.

The enthusiasm shown for these contests by thousands of teachers[2] throughout the United States has been highly encouraging. The number of student entries in the contests has[3] increased approximately 25 per cent each year.

The Capital Pen Company presents gold cups to the[4] teachers who enter the wining classes. A Capital fountain pen, equipped with a special shorthand point, is presented[5] to each student who is a member of a winning class.

The enclosed folder describes in detail the rules[6] and awards of this year's contest. We should be most happy to welcome your class in this competition. Yours truly,[7]

571. Dear Principal: Since June, 1945, Bruce College has annually awarded high school honor scholarships[8] to outstanding graduates of recognized secondary schools. These awards amount to $500,[9] one-fourth of the student's tuition over a period of four years. The student thus receives the equivalent[10] of one year of college free, so far as tuition is concerned.

The top-ranking student in a class of 15[11] to 50 members is eligible. In classes of 51 to 100 members, the two top-ranking[12] students are eligible; and the top three in classes of more than 100 members would qualify.

When the[13] necessary information is available, will you kindly make your recommendations on the enclosed[14] card and return it.

For further information, consult "A Handbook for High School Counselors." Very cordially yours,[15] (300)

READING AND WRITING PRACTICE

572.

, parenthetical

, apposition
girls'
accepted

modernly
, nonrestrictive
, parenthetical

: enumeration
, series
linen

, conjunction

, if clause
racket

, apposition
 inside quote

, series
articles
religious

Women's
Self-Government

573.

; no conjunction
, introductory

eyesight
, series
, introductory

[Shorthand content]

accommodate
various
, parenthetical

tomorrow's
citizens

574.

up to date
  no noun,
  no hyphen
, *and* omitted

, introductory

probability
, introductory
; illustrative ,

[shorthand]

, introductory
separate
offered

[shorthand]

, *as* clause

[shorthand]

, parenthetical
bulletins
describing

[shorthand]

575.

[shorthand]

worth-while
hyphenated
before noun

[shorthand]

describes

[shorthand]

LESSON 78

576. USEFUL BUSINESS-LETTER PHRASES

UNDERSTAND

UNDERSTOOD

INTERSECTION

GEOGRAPHICAL PHRASES

Key

I understand, to understand, we understand, who understand, he understands, she understands, they understand, I can understand.

I understood, he understood, we understood, who understood, it is understood.

Associated Press, a.m., p.m., Chamber of Commerce, vice versa.

Boston, Massachusetts; Denver, Colorado; Memphis, Tennessee; Chicago, Illinois.

577. FREQUENT NAMES

a.

b.

Key

a. Thomas, Thompson, Thomson, Turner, Walker, Walsh.
b. Samuel, Stephen, Vincent, Walter, William.

CHAPTER XVI

578. PREVIEW AND WRITING PRACTICE

PREVIEW FOR LETTER **579.**

PREVIEW FOR LETTER **580.**

Key

Sectional, Atlantic, speaker, annual.

Ideal, to serve, you would be able, to make, contribution, to our, including, two o'clock.

Pleasure, accept, invitation, calendar.

Presume, exact, basic, observations, especially, period, conclusions, acceptance.

579. Dear Mr. Price: As chairman of the Business Education Sectional Meeting of the Atlantic Education[1] Association, it is my job to obtain a speaker for our annual meeting. Mr. Roy Sears, sales[2] representative of the Brown Publishing Company, has suggested you as an ideal person to serve as[3] our speaker this year. He felt that you would be able to make an important contribution to our meeting.

The[4] Atlantic Education Association will hold its annual meeting this year on Friday, February[5] 6. The sectional meetings, including ours in business education, start at two o'clock in the afternoon.[6]

After receiving Mr. Sears's suggestion, I talked with Doctor Warner, professor of Business Education[7] at our state college. He also agreed that you would be an excellent person to talk to our group.

Doctor[8] Warner and I both thought that a panel discussion on some of the issues brought out in your speech would be worth while.[9]

Will you please write to me as soon as possible whether you would be willing to appear on our program. Yours truly,[10]

580. Dear Miss Hansen: It is a pleasure to accept your invitation to speak at your meeting on February[11] 6. I have marked this date on my calendar. I presume that at some later date you will let me know the exact[12] time and place.

One topic, "Some Basic Observations in Business Education," appeals to me especially.[13] These are some observations that I have made over a period of twenty-five years and on which I have come[14] to some definite conclusions.

I am sending a copy of this acceptance to Doctor Warner. Yours truly,[15] (300)

READING AND WRITING PRACTICE

581.

, apposition
appropriate

experiences
keenly

; no conjunction
, introductory

582.

[shorthand]

, nonrestrictive

[shorthand]

; because of comma
, *if* clause
lookout

[shorthand]

connections
materialize

[shorthand]

583.

, apposition
   inside quote
12-page
   hyphenated
   before noun
, series

[shorthand]

, *if* clause

[shorthand]

584.

, apposition
ballot

level
Committee
, introductory

, nonrestrictive
inside quote

, *as* clause
candidacy
co-workers

tomorrow
appreciated

585.

CHAPTER XVI

, parenthetical

; because of comma
, *when* clause
preparation

, introductory
remind

, introductory
. inside quote

year's
predecessors

, *if* clause

LESSON 79

586. WORD ENDINGS

-WARD

-RITY

-LITY

-IFICATION

-MENTAL

-HOOD

Key

Awkward, awkwardly, awkwardness, forward, forwarded, reward, rewarded.

Alacrity, popularity, similarity, mediocrity, severity.

Reality, cordiality, neutrality, partiality, triviality.

Falsification, diversification, identification, gratification, verification, classification.

Ornamental, temperamental, sentimental, monumental.

Falsehood, statehood, likelihood, livelihood, bachelorhood.

CHAPTER XVI

587. PREVIEW AND WRITING PRACTICE

PREVIEW FOR LETTER **588.**

PREVIEW FOR LETTER **589.**

Key

There has been, demand, businessmen, self-improvement, ability.
Language, outlines, retention, enrich, enjoyment, associated, capacity.
Leadership, anyone, studying, next time, practical, values.
Announcement, shortly, publications, duplicating.
Processes, prepared, descriptive, brochure, compliments, simply, postage.

588. Dear Mr. Green: Dr. Glenn Gray has written a book for which there has been a great demand from businessmen for many[1] years. His book, "Reading for Self-Improvement," shows you how you can improve your reading ability.

In simple[2] language, Doctor Gray outlines a working plan that will greatly increase your reading speed, improve your retention, and[3] enrich the enjoyment you will obtain from reading.

Reading is a skill so closely associated with a[4] person's capacity for leadership that its importance cannot be stressed too strongly. Anyone can reap the[5] benefits of improved reading skill by studying "Reading for Self-Improvement." Ask to see a copy the next[6] time you are in your favorite bookstore. An even better idea would be to mail us your check for $3.[7] It will bring you a practical book that will increase the many values to be obtained from reading. Yours truly, [8]

589. Dear Friend: Because of your interest in modern business-training methods, I thought you would like to have the enclosed[9] advance proof of an announcement that will appear shortly in business-education publications.

The announcement[10] describes a newly developed program for the teaching of duplicating processes. Prepared by Dr.[11] Fred Lawrence, the eight-lesson course has been designed to answer the expressed needs of business teachers all over the[12] country. The course is organized to make your job easier.

We have a descriptive brochure that gives further details[13] on this course in the teaching of the duplicating processes. I should like to mail you a copy with my compliments.[14] To obtain this brochure, simply fill in the enclosed postage-paid card and drop it in the mail. Yours truly,[15] (300)

READING AND WRITING PRACTICE

590.

, *as* clause
, introducing short quote

, *if* clause inside quote
question

, introductory
vacancies
elementary

, *if* clause

, parenthetical
; no conjunction
, introductory

experience
invaluable
, if clause

corps
total

quality
convenience

591.

, conjunction

considerable
eager
conference

, apposition
Transcribe:
  8:30 a.m.

, *when* clause
participate

, introductory
assigned

, parenthetical
pleasant

592.

everywhere
. inside quote

; illustrative ,
, series

CHAPTER XVI

, introductory
bookshelf

593.

artist's
scientist's
, series

, series

: enumeration
textbooks
, nonrestrictive

up to date
no noun,
no hyphen

476

LESSON 80

594. WORD-BUILDING PRACTICE — OMISSION OF VOWELS

-TATION, ETC.

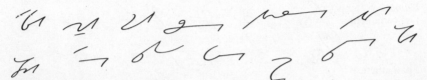

OMISSION OF MINOR VOWEL

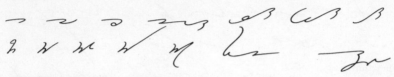

-EST FOLLOWING A VOWEL

Key

Transportation, quotation, foundation, examination, discrimination, destination, repetition, reputation, transmission, additional, permission, combination, admission.

New, newer, newly, numerous, reduce, produce, induce, issue, suit, suits, suited, suitable, volume, manufacture.

Handiest, neediest, greediest, narrowest, slowest, costliest.

595. ACCURACY PRACTICE — SIMILAR OUTLINES

a.

b.

Key

a. You, this, way, say, we, see, you will, it will, you are, to our.
b. They, to me, that, with, when, yet, I think, I can, he can.

READING AND WRITING PRACTICE

596. Secretarial Work

glamour
; no conjunction

, parenthetical
, *if* clause

, conjunction
  inside quote

, series
initiative

, series
occasionally

company's

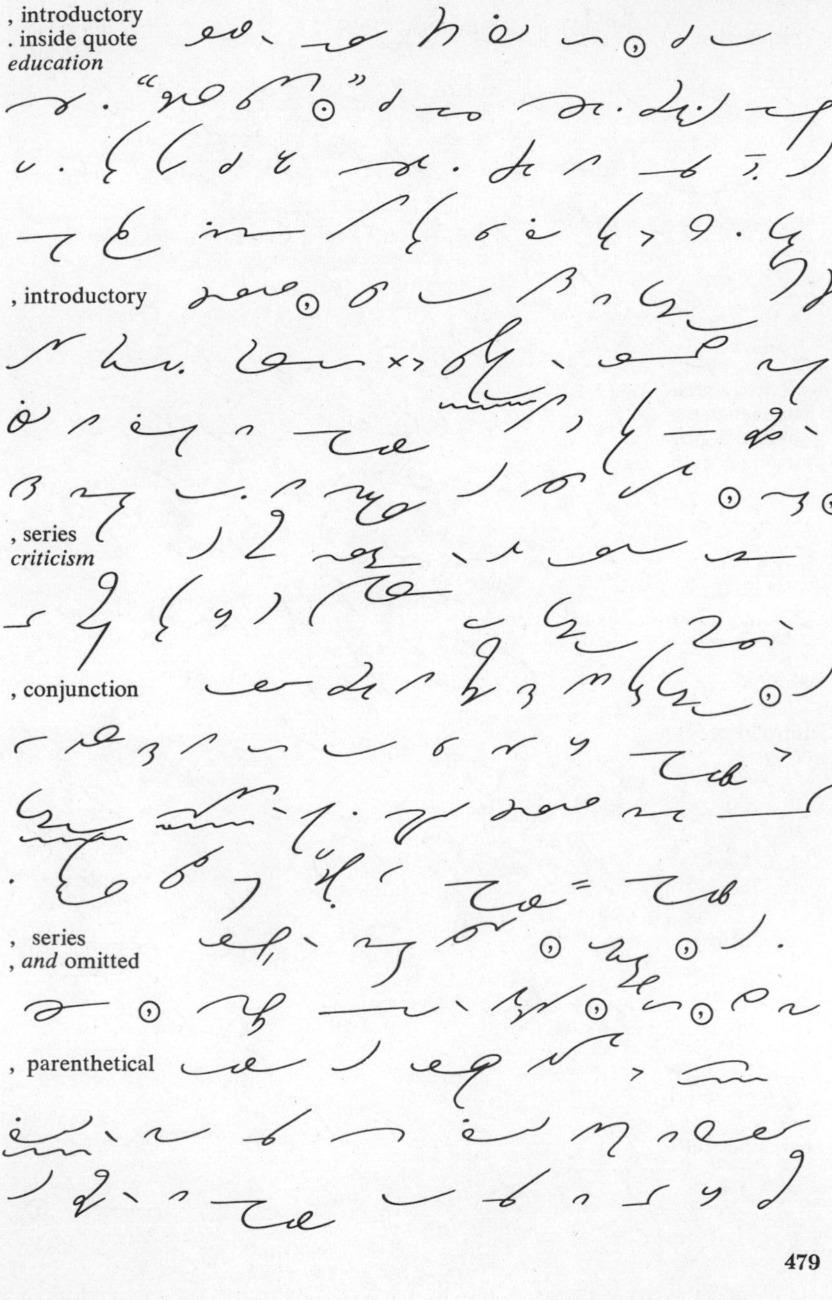
, introductory
. inside quote
education
, introductory
, series
criticism
, conjunction
, series
, *and* omitted
, parenthetical

, conjunction

[shorthand]

well-modulated
hyphenated
before noun
, introductory

[shorthand]

, introductory
accept

[shorthand]

, introductory

[shorthand]

, series
, parenthetical

[shorthand]

municipal
, series

Mayors
, series

, series
charities
noncommercial

, series
, nonrestrictive
receptionists

, parenthetical
, series
laboratory

CHAPTER XVI

(6)

, conjunction
wholesale
advancement

(8)

aviation
, series

, series

, *as* clause
, introductory

MARGINAL REMINDERS EXPLAINED

In the following pages you will find more complete statements of the principles of punctuation and other transcription aids briefly indicated in the marginal reminders of this book. It is not intended that you should attempt to learn these principles; they are presented here as an aid to the understanding of the marginal reminders. Your ability to apply the principles will come from the constant repetition of the reminders in the margin.

The main purpose of the transcription punctuation reminders given in the margins of this text is to help you get the "knack" of punctuating the constructions most frequently used in ordinary business correspondence. For that reason (and because of the obvious necessity for extreme brevity), the reminders have been made so short and so simple that the grammarian might well quarrel with the wording of some of them. In this section each of the very brief reminders is discussed more fully and with a careful explanation of the grammatical relationships involved. It is more important, however, that you form the habit of correctly punctuating these simple business constructions than that you be able to give the complete and accurate grammatical explanation.

The headings given below are the same as those used in the marginal reminders.

1. , parenthetical

In order to make his meaning clearer, a writer sometimes inserts a comment or explanation that could be omitted without changing the meaning of the sentence. These added comments and explanations are called parenthetical and are separated from the rest of the sentence by parentheses, dashes, or commas.

> You, too, will not be able to resist ordering from our catalogue.
> Do you, however, budget carefully?

A special type of parenthetical expression is called apposition and is explained below.

2. , apposition

Sometimes a writer mentions a certain person or thing and then, in order to make his meaning perfectly clear to the reader, says the same thing in different words.

> The San Francisco Limited, another of our trains, did make a stop at Riverside.
> The meeting will be held on Wednesday, March 15, at ten o'clock.

In many cases these constructions in apposition resemble the constructions in which the commas are used to set off parenthetical expressions. It is really immaterial whether the transcriber thinks he is using the commas to set off an apposition or to set off a parenthetical expression. These expressions are substantially the same thing and the result is identical.

An apposition may occur at the end of a sentence, in which case only one comma is needed.

> He will be in your city on Monday, February 26.

3. , series

When three or more similar expressions (words, phrases, or clauses) occur in a series with a conjunction before the last expression, a comma should be placed before the conjunction.

> Your merchandise is of the finest quality, your prices are fair, and your service is unexcelled.
> You will be especially interested in the suits, dresses, and shoes shown in the catalogue.
> A sincere smile, a spirit of friendliness, and a desire to be helpful are indications of courtesy.

4. , introductory
5. , if clause
6. , when clause
7. , as clause

One of the most frequent errors made by the beginning transcriber is the failure to make a complete sentence. In most cases the incomplete sentence is a dependent, or subordinate, clause introduced by *if, when,* or *as.* The dependent, or subordinate, clause deceives the transcriber because it seems to be a complete sentence, when actually it is a clause introduced by a word such as *if* or *as* and therefore requires a main (independent) clause to complete the thought. If . . . *what?* When . . . *what?*

The dependent, or subordinate, clause signals the coming of another clause with a relative pronoun or a subordinate conjunction. The relative pronouns are *that, who, what, which, whoever, whatever, whichever.* The commonest subordinating conjunctions are *if, though, although, whether, unless, as, because, when, since, while, where, after, wherever, until, before, how, however.*

In this text each *if* clause, *when* clause, and *as* clause has been marked as such in the margin because these are by far the three commonest subordinating conjunctions found in business correspondence.

> If you are holding this package, will you please let us know.
> When your trunk arrives at the railroad station, we will have it delivered immediately.
> As we stated in our previous correspondence, we want these men to observe the process in the manufacture of paper.

The other and less frequent dependent clauses have been grouped under the general marginal reminder ", introductory."

> By keeping the cash registers of America ringing, he also keeps our factories humming.

Once customers have made their selection of merchandise, they should be given quick service.
In order to find a solution to this problem, we must ask for your co-operation.

The rule covering the group of introductory dependent clauses is that a comma is used to separate a subordinate clause from a *following* main clause. If the main clause comes first, no comma is required. A comma was placed in the preceding sentence after the subordinate clause (*if the main clause comes first*) because that clause came before the main clause. No comma would be required if the position of the two clauses were reversed so that that sentence would read: *No comma is required if the main clause comes first*.

Thus the comma is required when the subordinate clause introduces the main clause. Similarly, a comma is required after other introductory or explanatory expressions, such as *on the contrary, in brief, for instance*.

With the advent of the supermarket, methods of retailing have changed.
Generally, these trips are to our branch factories.
Furthermore, it would be most unusual to stop this train for the purpose of discharging passengers.

You will find it safe to use a comma after any introductory or explanatory expression or after any element of a sentence that is used at the beginning of the sentence out of its natural word order. The writer whose judgment has been formed by constant practice will often prefer to omit the comma after a short introductory expression that seems to flow into the rest of the sentence without a break.

The constant observation of good models is the best and surest way to become proficient in the art of punctuation. In this text you will have called to your attention by the marginal reminders hundreds of examples of the correct punctuation of introductory or explanatory elements at the beginning of the sentence under the four headings discussed in this section.

8. , nonrestrictive

Nonrestrictive clauses and phrases are set off by commas. A nonrestrictive clause or phrase is one that may be omitted without changing the meaning of the sentence. The nonrestrictive clause or phrase might be classified as parenthetical. It is important that you follow the meaning of the transcript in order to be able to identify the restrictive and the nonrestrictive clauses and phrases and to punctuate them correctly.

> Restrictive — no commas: The automobile that was speeding was completely destroyed.
> Nonrestrictive — commas: The automobile, which was speeding, was completely destroyed.

In the first sentence above *that was speeding* is a restrictive clause and must not be set off by commas. The expression *that was speeding* identifies the particular automobile that was destroyed. In the second sentence, *which was speeding* is a nonrestrictive or descriptive or parenthetical clause that must be set off with commas. It does not identify the particular automobile that was destroyed; it merely describes further an automobile that has already been identified. Notice in the foregoing examples that the careful writer uses *that* to introduce a restrictive clause and *which* to introduce a nonrestrictive clause. Many dictators fail to observe this distinction, however.

The rules for using commas apply likewise to restrictive and nonrestrictive phrases.

> Restrictive — no commas: The girl standing in the garden waved to him.
> Nonrestrictive — commas: The girl, standing in the garden, waved to him.

In the first of the preceding sentences, *standing in the garden* is a restrictive phrase and must not be set off with commas. The expression *standing in the garden* identifies the particular girl who waved to him. In the second sentence, *standing in the garden* is a nonrestrictive or descriptive or parenthetical phrase that must be set off with commas. It does not identify the girl who waved. The girl has already been identified by a previous sentence or by a gesture of the speaker; the nonrestrictive phrase *standing in the garden* merely describes where she stood when she waved.

The use of the commas is determined by the meaning of the sentence. You can always tell the dictator's meaning by the inflection of his voice during dictation. Even though you have neglected to make the proper indication in your shorthand notes, it is almost always possible to decide from the context of the dictation whether an expression was intended to be nonrestrictive or restrictive — whether it should be transcribed with or without commas.

9. , and omitted

Usually two adjectives preceding a noun are separated by a comma.

> You can send your answers to us in the stamped, self-addressed envelope provided.

The comma is not used if the first adjective modifies the second adjective and the noun as a unit.

> She wore a beautiful green dress.

10. , conjunction
11. ; no conjunction

Although in some ways this is one of the easiest punctuation problems, and certainly one of the most frequent, few beginning transcribers seem to be able to solve it rapidly and accurately.

The first of the preceding headings represents a brief reminder that a comma is used to separate two independent clauses that are joined by one of the conjunctions *and, but, or, for, neither, nor*. If the two independent clauses are not joined by one of those conjunctions, the clauses are separated by a semicolon.

An independent clause (sometimes called a *main* or *principal* clause) is one that has a subject and predicate and could stand alone as a separate sentence.

> We believe you will enjoy going through these questions, and I am sure you will feel that you have gained much useful information after you have done so.

The first independent or principal or main clause is

> We believe you will enjoy going through these questions . . .

because that clause could stand as a separate sentence. The second independent clause, which could also stand as a separate sentence, is

> . . . I am sure you will feel that you have gained much useful information after you have done so.

These clauses could be written as two separate sentences with a period after each. Because the thought of the two sentences is closely related, it seemed better to the writer of the letter to put them into one sentence. Because the two independent clauses are connected by the co-ordinating conjunction *and,* a comma is used between them. The writer could have said:

> We believe you will enjoy going through these questions; I am sure you will feel that you have gained much useful information after you have done so.

In this case the semicolon would be used to separate the two independent clauses because there is no conjunction.

In the marginal reminders there is no room for all this explanation. Therefore, when you see in the margin

> , conjunction

it is a reminder that the comma is used between the two independent clauses because they are separated by one of the co-ordinating conjunctions *and, but, or, for, neither, nor.* When you see in the margin

; no conjunction

it is a reminder that the semicolon is used between the two independent clauses because they are not separated by one of the six conjunctions just listed. In such sentences you may remember that you should not use a semicolon unless you could just as correctly use a period and divide the one sentence into two sentences.

The source of most of the confusion and difficulty is the use of the semicolon that is explained in the next section.

12. ; because of comma

If the comma were always used between independent clauses connected by a conjunction, and if the semicolon were always used between independent clauses not connected by a conjunction, the learner would have little trouble becoming accustomed to the correct punctuation. The one exception referred to by the preceding heading serves to confuse the learner. The exception is that the semicolon is used instead of the comma if a comma is used within either of the independent clauses joined by a conjunction.

The reason for this change from comma to semicolon seems simple enough. If there are other commas in the sentence, something stronger than a comma is required to separate the two parts of the sentence.

The following sentence, for example, uses a comma to separate the two independent clauses joined by the conjunction *and*:

> We believe you will enjoy going through these questions, and I am sure you will feel that you have gained much useful information after you have done so.

When the sentence is changed by the addition of one word and a comma, as shown below, the comma after *questions* must be changed to a semicolon.

> Consequently, we believe you will enjoy going through
> these questions; and I am sure you will feel that you
> have gained much useful information after you have
> done so.

It is clear that the punctuation between the two independent clauses, the two main parts of the sentence, must be of greater strength than the punctuation within the first clause. Therefore, the semicolon is used instead of the comma.

Such a sentence should present no problem to the transcriber because the comma occurs in the first clause. The good transcriber, however, must keep his eyes several words ahead of his fingers, because often the comma will occur in the second clause. Here is the same sentence with a parenthetical phrase added in the second clause, necessitating the change from a comma to a semicolon before the *and*:

> We believe you will enjoy going through these ques-
> tions; and I am sure, Mr. Smith, you will feel that you
> have gained much useful information after you have
> done so.

The transcriber might put a comma after *questions* unless he had already read far enough to notice the parenthetical expression in the second clause.

Sometimes the marginal reminder

> ; no conjunction

is used for a sentence in which the semicolon is used primarily because no conjunction joins the two independent clauses but in which it would have been used in any event because of the presence of commas within one or both the independent clauses.

Comparative Review of Uses of Comma and Semicolon

1. Comma between preceding dependent (subordinate) clause and following independent (main) clause:

> If we are to meet our bills, we must collect what is
> due from our customers.

491

2. No punctuation at all if the dependent (subordinate) clause comes after the main clause:

> We must collect what is due from our customers if we are to meet our bills.

3. Comma between two independent (main) clauses joined by the conjunctions *and, but, or, for, neither, nor*:

> We have to meet our bills, but we cannot do so until we collect what is due from our customers.

4. Semicolon between two independent (main) clauses joined by the conjunctions *and, but, for, or, neither, nor* if there is a comma in either clause:

> a. Moreover, we have to meet our bills; but we cannot do so until we collect what is due from our customers.
> b. We have to meet our bills; but we cannot do so, as a practical matter, until we collect what is due from our customers.
> c. Moreover, we have to meet our bills; but we cannot do so, as a practical matter, until we collect what is due from our customers.

5. Semicolon between two independent (main) clauses that are not joined by the conjunctions *and, but, or, for, neither, nor*:

> We have to meet our bills; we cannot do so until we collect what is due from our customers.

13. ; illustrative ,

When an illustration is introduced by some such expression as *namely* or *that is,* the expression should be preceded by a semicolon and followed by a comma.

> Food for your students can be obtained on the train by means of two different types of accommodations; namely, complete meals in the dining car or light lunches at the snack counter.

14. : enumeration

A colon is used after an expression that is an introduction to some following material, such as a long quotation, an explanation of a general statement, a list, or an enumeration.

> There are three requirements: speed, accuracy, and artistry.
> The new plate has this advantage: you can use it in any of the ten stores listed on the enclosed card.

15. The Apostrophe

No attempt has been made to explain the reason for each apostrophe noted in the marginal reminders. The transcriber nearly always knows the reason but simply doesn't remember to use the apostrophe. This book provides the learner with many reminders of the correct use of the apostrophe.

16. Quotations

Several transcription usages in regard to the transcribing of quotations are summarized under this heading.

1. Short quotations are introduced by a comma.

> The boy said, "Help me, sir."

2. Long quotations are introduced by a colon.

> The boy said: "I have studied for many years to prepare for this work, and I hope that you are willing to help me find a place either here or in some neighboring city."

3. The comma and the period are always typed inside the final quotation mark; other punctuation marks are placed inside or outside the final quotation mark, according to the sense of the sentence.

> "I cannot believe," she said, "that he has left."
> She asked, "Why did he go?"
> Why did she say, "He has left"?

17. Hyphenated before noun
18. No noun, no hyphen
19. No hyphen after ly

The presence or absence of the hyphen in expressions like *worth while* and *up to date* causes transcription errors largely because of the infrequency of the problem. The principle is extremely simple. If a noun follows the expression, the hyphens are inserted — no following noun, no hyphen.

> The book is up to date. (No noun after the expression.)
> The up-to-date book . . . (Noun follows the expression.)

An exception, which sometimes confuses the learner, is that no hyphen is used when the first element of the modifier ends in *ly*. Therefore, there would be no hyphen in *skillfully planned campaign*.

20. Dates

Although there are a large number of dates in the letters, only a few of them have been put in the margins as reminders that the correct form is *March 20*, without the *th* after the figure.

The year figure is set off by commas.

> It was in June, 1949, that I first met him.

21. Figures

The correct form for transcribing even amounts of dollars is *$83* with no decimal point and no ciphers.

> . . . remittance of $25 or return the merchandise.
> . . . your overdue account of $25.
> The amount, as you know, is $166; and . . .

As you can see in the foregoing examples, sometimes the figures representing the amount will be followed by a period, a semicolon, or another mark of punctuation required by the context of the sentence.

Amounts indicating *cents* and *per cent* are written as shown in the following examples. *Per cent* is written as two words without a following period, but *percentage* is one word.

It is true that 98 per cent of the items may be purchased for 7 cents or less.

Some of the amounts are noted in the margin as reminders; many of them are not, as their mere presence in the letter serves as a reminder.

22. . courteous request

This usage is seldom found except in business correspondence. The businessman is always trying to persuade the customer or prospective customer to take some action desired by the businessman. The customer might take offense if the businessman were to say directly, *I want to hear from you by return mail*. Therefore, the businessman says:

May we hear from you by return mail.

Attention is called to these requests in the margin, to give you many reminders of the difference between a question and a courteous request. The question must be followed by a question mark; the courteous request, by a period.

You may remember that the courteous request always calls for an answer in the form of an action; the question calls for an answer in the form of words.

The businessman who said *May we hear from you by return*

mail did not expect the answer to be *yes*. He expected the answer to be a letter by return mail.

> The small things are the ones that we overlook, aren't they?

The question mark is used in the foregoing sentence because the only possible answer would be the word *yes*.

23. Spelling and Capitalization

Words that present any difficulty in spelling or capitalization are correctly printed in the margin. Certain of them occur many times in the course of the text. This constant repetition in the natural context is more successful in teaching material of this sort than the most intensive study of any one form at a time.

RECALL DRILLS

List of Joined Word Endings

1. -MENT

2. -LESS

3. -TION

4. -TIAL

5. -LY

6. -ILY, -ALLY

7. -POSE, -POSITION

8. -IFY

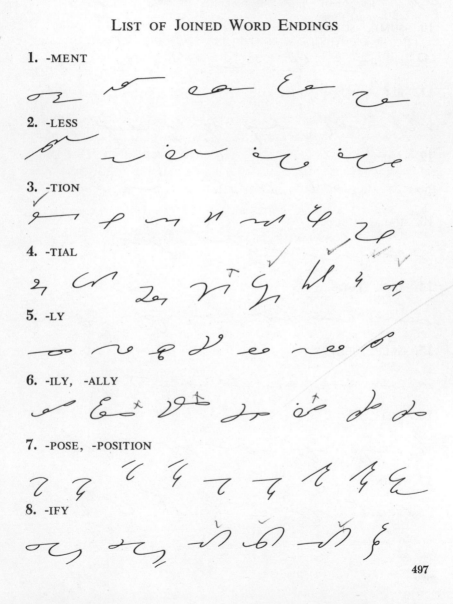

APPENDIX

9. -FUL

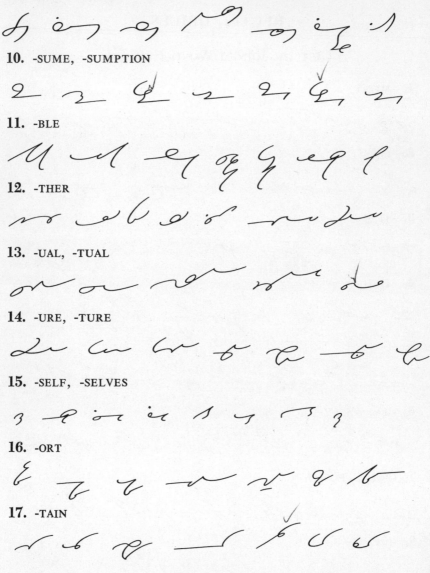

10. -SUME, -SUMPTION

11. -BLE

12. -THER

13. -UAL, -TUAL

14. -URE, -TURE

15. -SELF, -SELVES

16. -ORT

17. -TAIN

LIST OF DISJOINED WORD ENDINGS

18. -HOOD

19. -WARD

20. -SHIP

21. -CLE, -CAL

22. -ULATE

23. -INGLY

24. -INGS

25. -GRAM

26. -IFICATION

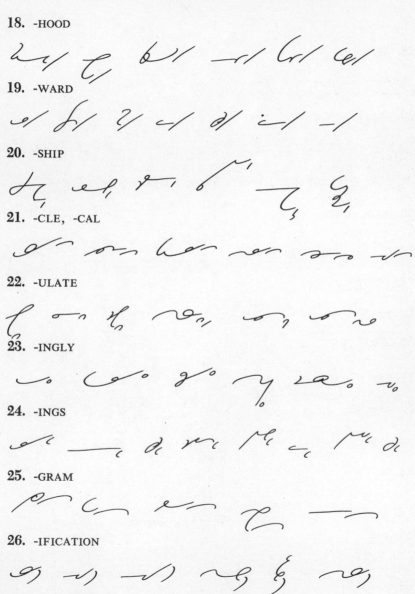

27. -LITY

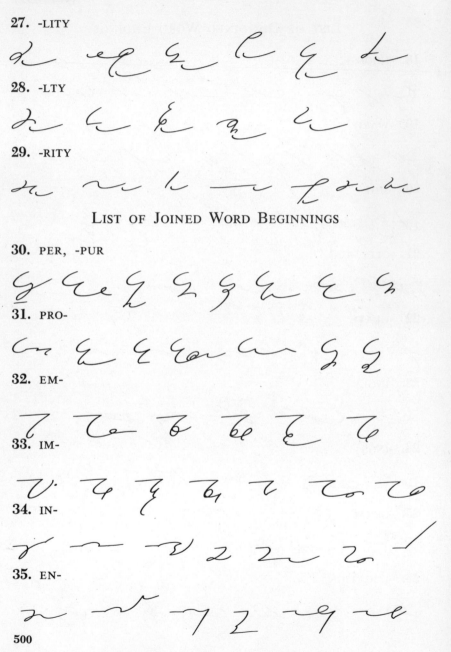

28. -LTY

29. -RITY

List of Joined Word Beginnings

30. PER, -PUR

31. PRO-

32. EM-

33. IM-

34. IN-

35. EN-

36. UN-

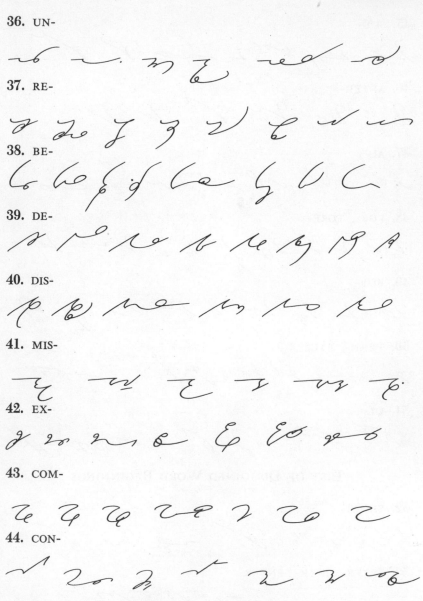

37. RE-

38. BE-

39. DE-

40. DIS-

41. MIS-

42. EX-

43. COM-

44. CON-

APPENDIX

45. SUB-

46. AFTER-

47. AL-

48. FOR-, FORE-

49. FUR-

50. TERN-, ETC.

51. UL

List of Disjoined Word Beginnings

52. SHORT-

53. INTER-, INTR-, ENTER-

54. ELECTR-, ELECTRIC

55. POST-

56. SUPER-, SUPR-

57. CIRCUM-

58. SELF-

59. TRANS-

60. INCL-

61. SHIP-

62. UNDER-

63. OVER-

LIST OF SPECIAL PHRASES

64. TO OMITTED BEFORE DOWNSTROKE

65. BEEN REPRESENTED BY B

66. ABLE REPRESENTED BY A

67. WANT PRECEDED BY PRONOUN

68. AGO REPRESENTED BY G

69. WAS NOT, IS NOT

70. UNDERSTAND, UNDERSTOOD

71. TO OMITTED IN PHRASES

72. THE OMITTED IN PHRASES

73. OF OMITTED IN PHRASES

74. AND OMITTED IN PHRASES

75. A OMITTED IN PHRASES

76. SPECIAL PHRASES